BOLTER

Bolter

Nieta Van Bladel

First edition published 2025 by Phoenix Books
Copyright © 2025 Nieta Van Bladel
The moral right of the author has been asserted in accordance with the Copyright, Designs and Patents Act 1988.
All rights reserved.
No part of this book may be reproduced, stored, or transmitted by any means—whether auditory, graphic,
mechanical, or electronic—without written permission of both publisher and author, except in the case of
brief excerpts used in critical articles and reviews. Unauthorized reproduction of any part of this work is illegal and is punishable by law.
This novel is entirely a work of fiction. The names, characters and incidents portrayed are the work of the author's imagination. Any resemblances to actual persons, living or dead, events or localities are entirely coincidental.

Cover Design: Jayden Morgan
Interior Layout: Pickawoowoo Publishing Group
Printing & Distribution Channel: IngramSpark / Lightning Source

First Edition: December, 2025
For more information or to book an event, e-mail enquiries to: nieta.vb@hotmail.com

 A catalogue record for this book is available from the National Library of Australia

ISBN: 978-0-9945937-4-0 (Paperback)

1

Hilda Wendelin Perry had to stand on tippy toes and balance herself precariously on the top rung of her ancient ladder just to reach the last wood box of hops. She wasn't sure why the regulars at her Pig and Port Inn had recently increased their thirst for her father's famous ale of late. Perhaps life was becoming somewhat tedious in Portsmouth, and the only solution was to drink themselves into a soggy oblivion. Obviously, the freezing weather played a large part in dampening one's mood. The lack of affordable warm housing was another reason for sure. Her father had left strict instructions on his passing that if she was going to make a success of keeping his beloved Inn open and all bums on seats, she would have to keep the fires stoked high to bring the patrons in.

When her father's health had started to falter, he had been unsure of granting her wish to keep the Tudor style corner Inn open. It was hard enough for a woman in 1820 to survive in the world, let alone run a business in what should surely stay a predominately male domain. She couldn't work out the front, he had reminded her. Women were not allowed to be *behind* the bar and serving the delicious amber broth. Irrelevant of the fact that on the other side of the bar it was perfectly acceptable for the lushy coves and covesses, as he called his heavy drinking clientele, to be associating. He knew his daughter had a fine art in the making of the strong ale; she had practically grown up in the back of the pub, getting under his feet and asking all sorts of bothersome questions. But she was as stubborn as her dearly departed mother, God rest her soul, so he had endured her curiosity and taught her his craft.

Indeed, he had told her on numerous occasions that "the intent of every brewer, when he forms his drink, is to extract the fermentable part of the malt, in the most perfect manner, to add hops, in such a proportion as experience teaches him will preserve and ameliorate the beer; and to employ just as much yeast as is sufficient to obtain a complete fermentation."

It wasn't until Hilda had begun to read and write that she came across that exact verse in her father's most treasured book; The Theory and Practice of Brewing 1804, that she realised her father had quoted word for word from page two, and that perhaps he wasn't as well-spoken as she had first admired.

What had made her father relent in the end was the promise from his most trusted Brewer, Angus Drew, that he would surely stick around and make sure Mrs Perry made a fair go of her venture. Angus was indispensable during the early days of setting up the Inn, although just a young lad at the time, he came with a generous amount of knowledge in the craftmanship of brewing, having been taught by his grandfather before him. He was a tall, strong young man that could easily handle the heavy lifting for the copper boiler, the mash tubs and underbacks. Precise on the thermometers and fermentables, and both genial and controlled during service, he had proven himself time and again. And most of all, having grown up together, his loyalty to Hilda was unwavering.

So, at age 50, having raised her now married daughter and dealing with the day to day running of her middle-class life, Hilda had told, rather than asked, her pompous lazy husband that she would be taking on the duties of full-time brewer of both the lager and the wine. Her ambition was to make the most brisk and agreeable spirituous fluids from fermented vegetable bodies this side of London.

2

Angus burst into the distillery room by bashing the double doors open with the heavy wooden boxes he carried, laden with hessian sacks and kicking along a new empty wine barrel from the delivery cart in the back lane. He was cursing through his short beard about the lack of help around the place when he caught sight of Hilda on top of the ladder.

"Good lord woman! Get down from there, I told you I could get it." His voice was very deep and even with a slight note of frustration. While he loved working alongside Hilda, most days she drove him crazy with her stubbornness. He couldn't complain though, he *was* warned by her father of her relentless need to prove herself more than capable when it came to the heavy work.

Surprised by his sudden appearance and outburst Hilda lost her footing and began to wobble uncontrollably. She could feel the ladder coming away beneath her and looked around frantically for something to grab. She dropped the box of hops and wrapped both hands around the timber strut just as the ladder went crashing to the ground.

"Angus!" she bellowed, feeling the muscles pull in her shoulder blades.

"Calm down Hilda," he replied from under her. "Just let go and I'll catch you." His tone came out with a faint hint of humour.

"You best not be looking up my skirts Mr Drew. Taking advantage of a woman in desperate circumstances will have you dragged off to the colonies, I promise." Hilda had a smile on her face now and was glad he couldn't see it.

Angus had a chuckle to himself and spread out his arms, "Come on with you woman, I have a lot of beer to be making and can't be standing around here all day waiting for you to find some courage." He held back a laugh knowing that comment would have got Hilda going.

"Courage! I'll show you some bloody courage, you cheeky kincher." Hilda let go without so much of a heads up and regretted her actions immediately. She went down hard and fast before Angus was ready, knocking him to the ground with her body so that she lay across his stomach, and heard the wind rush from his lungs. Hilda was fine, he had broken her fall.

Hilda looked at Angus's face and saw he was smiling, all be it in a pained fashion, and she blushed wildly feeling her cheeks getting hot. Climbing off his body she smoothed down her high waisted wool dress and checked to make sure her breasts hadn't popped out of the low square neckline.

"Yes, well anyway. Let's get back to it then Angus, we've no time for lying about." She took one last look at him still laying on the floor, propped up on his elbows and smirking at her obvious discomfort, and stuck her proud chin in the air and stomped off.

Angus lay there until she had left the room, before raising himself and re-buttoning his cotton shirt, which had popped open during the fall, and put his flat cap beret back on his head. He cleared his mind of a thought that would never be a reality and carried on with his normal work. One batch of ale needed blackening because he wasn't happy with the colour yet, and there were two coppers in ebullition waiting on the first fermentables and worts. The fires under the coppers made the room hot and the mash tubs were ready for their first pounding.

He rolled up his sleeves and tied a bandanna around his brow to catch his sweat, and was just about to begin his work when William Perry marched through the distillery room. His high-collared linen shirt, tight-fitted trousers and button up waistcoat were pressed to perfection, looking like the proper gentry toff that he was. He interrupted Angus with a loud clearing of his throat while he slid his gloves off and put them in his top hat. Angus turned to William and held back on anything derogatory that he instinctively felt like saying.

"Mr Drew," William addressed Angus without making eye contact and proffered the hat and gloves imperiously. 'Where is my wife?"

'I believe she would be in the office, Mr Perry," Angus replied and did not take the hat. "As she is every day, sir, from morning till night."

Angus's jibe was ignored, and he watched the back of Mr Perry strut through to the inner office area. "Pidgeon-livered hornswoggle," Angus muttered under his breath and spat on the ground.

William Perry entered his wife's office without so much as a hello, helped himself to one of her fathers' sherries and promptly seated himself in the desk chair, putting his filthy boots up on the top. Hilda turned from her position at the filing cabinet and watched her husband go through his motions. He started moving paper around and closing open ledgers and all around just making a nuisance of himself.

"Hello dear," Hilda said after a deep inhale. "Is there something I can do for you?"

He ignored her for a moment and pretended to read a letter that was on her desk. Eventually he threw it to the side and looked up at her. "My dear. I have decided after much thought that we will need to hire another housekeeper. You are simply too busy here with your little Inn, and the sad few staff we do have need better organisation." He stood swiftly and turned his back on Hilda to look out the grimy window.

"I very much disagree, William. Mrs Dawson is more than capable at her station, and I haven't heard any complaints from the other staff." Hilda was extremely put out that he should make this her fault, the man did nothing all day except live off the money the Inn brought in and go socialise at his Men's Club. Hilda didn't even know what they did at the Men's Club, she had heard rumours, but surely not.

"I won't be arguing with you over this, Hilda." He put a hand up to silence her and continued looking out the window, "My mind is made up, and while I am still the man of the house what I say goes." He turned to look at her and she stepped back at his intensity.

"William, I must protest. I have everything very much under control, both here and at the house. We really can't afford another housemaid right now and..." Hilda trailed off as she watched her husband put on his gloves and hat.

At the door he turned to her and spoke in a deep threatening tone, "The matter is already dealt with."

Hilda watched William stride through the distillery and past Angus, who turned to look at her. She had her fists clenched and her jaw set. For too long now William had treated her with contempt. He had no interest in the Inn, apart from the handsome annual salary it paid him for being the man of the house. He had sailed along on Hildas father's coattails for the last twenty years and was happy to keep it going with her. He was not a particularly tall man nor overly attractive, but he was very smooth and told people what they wanted to hear to achieve his goals. He had an intensely large ego that needed constant grooming, which his mother usually could keep buoyant, but lately he had changed.

Now it was unprovoked nastiness towards Hilda and her Inn as if the building was to blame for her no longer being at his beck and call. At dinner parties he would talk and jest about the business being a hot spot for gibfaced old whores, wagtails and flapdoodles while she sat there, crimson faced and quiet. Hilda had even tried to push herself harder to be there for her husband by getting up earlier to achieve all the demands of running a business and to be home on time to supervise William's evening routine. He complained of the lack of intimacy between them, ignoring the fact that most nights Hilda fell asleep in the kitchen chair while organising the next day's servants' duties.

Hilda turned on her heels and walked back into her office and slammed the large oak door. She tried to breathe through her frustration but when she looked at the mud William had left on the desk, she threw her head back and screamed until she felt calm again. She patted down her already tidy dress and tucked a wayward flick of blonde hair back into its bun before opening the door to see Angus standing on the outside, looking worried.

"Are you alright, lass?" he asked carefully.

"Quite alright, Angus, thank you. Is there something you wanted?" She cleared her throat and raised her chin.

"Aye," he shuffled from foot-to-foot feeling this was not a good time. "It's time to load the bar for the evening, will you be wanting to count the barrels off before you go?"

"Not tonight, Angus," she cleared her throat again hearing it crack a little. "I have some urgent business to attend to at home. Could you possibly just tally it up for me yourself. Its only Monday after all. We can do a full restock tomorrow and I wanted to get some flags up around the bar to celebrate the new year coming in on the weekend. Something festive and uplifting to create a joyful drinking atmosphere." She had to look up to Angus's face because he was a good deal taller than she and saw care in his eyes, making her want to tell him all her woes. But instead, she dropped her face and looked away, remembering that she had to keep her feelings to herself. William had threatened her on many occasions to tell no one what went on in their private life.

"Aye," he said eventually. "That sounds like a good idea. I'll be getting on with it then." He stayed a little longer to see if she needed him before walking away and through the swinging door to the main bar.

Hilda packed her things to take home, muttering to herself as she threw the ledgers and books into her dear fathers wide-bottomed valise. How dare William overlord her decisions on the running of the household. How dare he even suggest she wasn't up to dealing with the servants. The gall of the idle man. Hilda left the Inn through the service door and wrapped her shawl tighter around her shoulders against the icy evening wind. She usually enjoyed the short walk home down the laneway and out onto the main street, admiring the fancy new gas streetlights that had recently been installed by the Portsea Improvement Commissioners. But not today. Something was up with William, something new, and she needed to get to the bottom of it.

3

Hilda approached the front of her family home, lost in her mood, and was surprised to see her housekeeper, Mrs Dawson, standing in the porch light looking nervous and wringing her hands in her handkerchief. Fearing the worst, Hilda picked up her pace until she was standing directly in front of Mrs Dawson and noticed she was near to tears.

"Come now, Mrs Dawson, it can't be as bad as that," Hilda comforted. "Come inside by the fire and we can talk."

"I'll not come inside, Mrs Perry. I need to speak with you alone and there is not a chance with that new big-eared Moll Myrtle hovering around listening to everything we say." Mrs Dawson looked embarrassed at her outpour.

"Moll Myrtle? Who is this Moll Myrtle you are speaking of?" Hilda looked over Mrs Dawsons shoulder and into the well-lit lounge room of the house. She could see William sitting by the large fire, his slippers already on his feet reading a paper with a smug look on his face.

"Mr Perry told us she is the new housekeeper, Mrs Perry. Am I to be let go after so many years working here?"

Hilda had to rub Mrs Dawsons arm to try and stop her bursting into tears. "Come now Mrs Dawson. I would never let that happen. Perhaps give me a moment to talk with Mr Perry and we will sort this whole mess out? Go make yourself a cup of tea." Hilda received an unsatisfied nod from Mrs Dawson and watched her walk away behind the building. "What in the devil is going on here?" she muttered to herself before opening the front door.

Hilda allowed the night maid to take her damp heavy coat and hat and noticed she was looking at Hilda with a pout. "Oh, not you too Mary, what is with you all tonight?"

"You'll see, miss," was all she said as she lowered her gaze and went about her business hanging the coat. Hilda's curiosity was now peaking as she walked through the foyer and into the lounge. The first thing she saw was a girl in her twenties standing behind her husband with her hand on his shoulder. She was dressed in a servants' outfit, but her familiarity with William was obvious. She took her hand away slowly and William followed her gaze to the door where Hilda stood.

"Ah, Hilda, you're home," he stated the obvious. His manner was jovial and pompous at the same time. Very unlike the William of late and it caught Hilda off guard.

'William," she spoke coldly while looking at the girl behind him. "I would like to speak with you. In private." Hilda kept her eyes on the girl and was furious to see her look down at William for confirmation to leave. "Now!" Hilda stormed further into the room until she was standing next to the girl looking her dead in the eyes. There was a mischievous, challenging look in those eyes that Hilda wanted to slap away, but she held her ground until the girl looked away and left the room. Hilda followed her and slammed the door behind her with enough force to rattle the side table. She waited a moment and then opened the door again to find the girl still standing there looking surprised. "That will be all thank you. You may collect your things and leave immediately. There has been some confusion, we do not require any more staff now." Hilda waited until the girl walked away, purposefully blocking her from looking into the room at William, who was now standing with his hands on his hips. She watched the girl leave through the front door and slammed it in her face.

"What are you doing Hilda. You had no right to treat poor Moll that way?" William had underestimated his wife's rage and shrunk back at the look in Hilda's eyes. "I mean she is such a nice girl; she was let go from the Men's Club and was terribly upset. She asked me if I could give her some work and I really thought you would be more understanding."

"Understanding!" Hilda was near hysterical. Did he actually think this was acceptable behaviour. Did he expect Hilda to have sympathy for that conniving, vasey hedge-creeper. Was the man that dumb? The thoughts going through her head were making her exhausted. "I'm going to bed now William," she said with a defeated sigh. "Perhaps we can discuss this further in the morning?" She looked at him one last time before she left the room and did not feel comforted by his scheming look.

Hilda entered the kitchen through the staff entrance and saw Mrs Dawson sitting at the table and the night maid hovering close by. They looked at her as she approached, and the maid offered her a cup of tea, which she declined and pointed to the wine bottle on the shelf. Hilda pulled out a chair and sat heavily, the glass of wine appearing before her immediately. She took a moment and had a sip, leaned her head back to stretch her neck, then focussed on Mrs Dawson sitting silently, staring at her.

"Ready when you are, Mrs Dawson, tell me everything you know about the girl."

Mrs Dawson immediately began rattling off information, both truth and gossip, declaring that the girl, Moll Myrtle, did indeed work at the Men's Club. Mrs Dawson crossed herself at the mention of the place, leading Hilda to believe it was indeed a place of ill repute, however Moll wasn't a prostitute Mrs Dawson added, but she was known around town as one not to be trusted around one's husband. She had been reportedly set to marry Old Lord Wexley before he died suddenly of a heart attack. Mrs Dawson and the night maid looked at each other and raised their eyebrows, making Hilda stop them before they went on another tangent of gossip. Hilda could only handle one scandal at a time tonight.

"So, we don't really know for sure if that is what is going on here, do we?" she asked, looking at them both through very tired eyes.

"We are just telling you what we know, Mrs Perry. We aren't suggesting a thing," the night maid responded for both the women, with innocence in her eyes. Yes, butter wouldn't melt in their mouths, Hilda thought to herself.

"Well, I have asked her to leave so that is the end of it then," Hilda yawned and stood to stretch. "Everything will be back to normal tomorrow. Good night, ladies."

Hilda dragged her tired body up to her room and found William already in the bed, fast asleep with that same smug smile on his face. What the devil was he up to? Hilda hated the unsettled feeling she had, so she walked around to William's side of the bed. His bedside cupboard had the top drawer slightly ajar, and the corner of an envelope was sticking out. Hilda looked one more time at William before sliding out the paper envelope and quietly opening it. It was addressed to William, in somewhat child-like handwriting, declaring a woman's love for him. She went on to say she understood how terrible his life must be with his horrible wife and that all he needed was a good woman to take care of him. She then declared she could be this woman if he so desired. It was signed Moll Myrtle.

Hilda was astounded. She could not move a muscle and just stood there staring at the letter. "He needs a good woman to look after him?" she whispered to herself in utter shock. "What the hell have I been doing for the last twenty years?" Hilda put the letter back in the envelope and slid it into her nightdress pocket. Her movements were slow, and her brain felt heavy with confusion.

She walked out of the bedroom and made her way to the guest room; she couldn't bear being anywhere near William right now, and she lacked the strength to start a fight. She walked like a zombie to the room, slid back the covers and got into the bed. She lay there feeling as though she wasn't in her own body anymore. Everything that she had thought to be true and real was now ripped out from under her, and anything that was white was now black. She fell asleep thinking she may just be in a dream.

4

Hilda left for the Inn while the morning was still dark and no one at the house had risen yet. She needed time to think about how she was going to deal with this situation. Fresh snow had fallen overnight, and her shoes sunk deeply with each step. Her woollen long coat and hat kept most of the chill out, but her face was turning red with the cold. As she neared the Inn, she stopped and admired the building in the streetlights warm glow. Built on the corner of Rose and Oliver Street, it looked cosy and inviting. The entrance was double oak doors with head-height, stained glass windows. The steep pitched gable roof and the original thatch covering made the dark, heavy timbers blend well with the whitewash walls and casement windows.

"Penny for your thoughts?" Angus said from behind Hilda, making her jump. Without thinking she put her arms around his neck and began weeping. Angus had no idea what was going on but her sobbing against his chest was worrying him. He held her until her body stopped and gently pulled her away from him. "What's happened Hilda, are you all right, lass?" He had to look close into her face because of the darkness, and he wiped a tear off her cheek with his thumb.

Hilda looked to the ground embarrassed by her behaviour. "Angus, I am so sorry, that was quite inappropriate of me. I have just had a rough night," she mumbled, stepping back from him and closing her coat tight. "I've just realised I have left something at home." She went to walk off and then stopped and turned. "I won't be long. Can you start the fires for me please?" and she gave him a small smile. "Thank you, Angus."

Angus watched her walk away, until she had turned the corner, and shivered. Something was wrong, terribly wrong. He put his hands into his pockets and walked the rest of the way to the building, deep in thought. She would be back soon, and he was determined to get it out of her then.

Hilda walked a few more paces then noticed several men standing under one of the streetlights. They were very heavy-set men, and a feeling of foreboding came over her. She quickened her pace, set her shoulders back to look more confident and walked on. The closer she got to them, the more she could make out their faces, and they were staring straight at her and smirking. Hilda looked to the other side of the road and contemplated crossing now. She was suddenly grabbed roughly by her arms, and she struggled to get free, but the men were so large she didn't have a chance. They started dragging her towards an alley, knocking off her hat as she struggled. She started to scream, and a smelly rag was put across her mouth and nose, so hard it made her eyes water. Slowly she felt herself falling asleep, her body going limp, and then there was nothing.

Hilda's body was roughly dragged further down the alley until they came to double barn doors. They knocked quietly and one of the doors was opened from the inside, creaking loudly on its rusty cold hinges.

"Put her over there," a small voice came from within.

Hilda's clothes were ripped roughly from her body, and a tattered rag of a dress was yanked over her head. They took off her silk stockings and heels and put her feet in old, scuffed boots. She was muddy now from the floor of the room, and her hair had come out of its bun.

"Take her away. Your money will be in the agreed place. Go quickly now before it is light."

5

Hilda woke feeling groggy and violently ill. There was a smell in the air of vomit and excrement, dirty bodies and urine. She sat suddenly and found herself lying on straw. Her stomach tightened and she gagged on the disgusting air. She looked around and saw that she was in a room with other women, all dressed in rags looking broken and lost. She was in a cell, and she didn't know how she'd gotten here. Looking down at her body, she saw she was dressed in rags as well, her hands and feet filthy with black muck. She started to panic, and her heart was racing so she stood and ran for the bars and started screaming. No one was there, no one was coming. A few of the women behind her started to curse her in whispers to be silent, but Hilda was out of her mind. Someone threw something at her back and her hair was grabbed from behind, yanking her back from the bars. She was thrown to the floor, and her cold hands and feet ached on the hard dirt. She looked up and saw a woman standing over her, with fiery red hair and a porcelain white complexion under the grime smeared across her face.

"You need to keep quiet girl!" she spat out in a whisper. "Any noise and you'll get the lot of us flogged." She looked to the prison bars, and all the women were dead silent, listening for footsteps.

Hilda looked around the room more carefully and noticed the look of fear in the women's faces.

The redhead grabbed an old lady's arm and spun her around so that Hilda could see the long blood stains that snaked the back of her garment.

"This is what you get for making a racket. Do you understand?" She pushed the woman away roughly and motioned for Hilda to be quiet. Everyone stayed like that for a few moments before they relaxed and started whispering to each other and staring at Hilda.

"What's your name?" the redhead asked.

"Hilda," she replied faintly, "Hilda Perry. Where am I?"

"My name is June, and you, my dear, are in the Watchhouse for delinquent women. I reckon you, being in here, dressed like that, should be a dandy story I would like to hear." She paused to sit next to Hilda and noticed all the other ladies were listening now. "Mind ya businesses ya nosey cows," she said, and the other women looked away.

"I honestly do not know why I am here. I was walking home, and two large men attacked me, dragged me into an alley, and put a rag across my nose and mouth. Then I woke up here," a sob escaped Hilda's mouth followed by several more, until she was having trouble breathing. June waited for her to calm down and frowned.

"You was jumped my dear, and I dare say you was drugged too." June was nodding to her own comment. "But why they put you in here is the confusing bit. Normally they just rape ya and throw you in the river." She looked at Hilda with concern. "Did they rape ya?" she asked, nodding down to Hilda's lap.

Hilda was looking at June with wide eyes of astonishment. "No, no I don't think so?"

"Yep, you'd know if they had," she noted, lapsing into thought again, while Hilda stared at her, shocked to be having such a conversation at all. "Was ya rich?" June eventually asked. "Was your husband well to do, I mean?"

Hilda stammered for a while, understanding where June was going with the conversation, and her mind went to William. But she sent the thought away immediately. William did not have the temerity to try something like this.

"You'll be called before the Judge soon, then you'll know," June said without sounding hopeful.

"Good, that is good. I can tell them there has been some sort of mistake." Hilda looked at June one more time and started to feel concerned.

There were footsteps coming down the hall now and all the ladies stood up and crept away from the door. They had gone silent again, and even June had a flash of fear cross her hazel eyes. "Keep ya mouth shut, woman, and only talk when they ask ya something. This Judge loves to see women getting a flogging, so do not give him any reason to. Do you hear me, Hilda?" June was holding Hilda's arm so tight it pinched, so she nodded, and they both stood up.

The guards came to the bars and called out, "Mary Cooper?" They looked around at all the women and said it again. No one answered. "It will be that new one," one of the guards pointed at Hilda, "Maybe she's deaf."

Hilda looked at June and saw she was looking back at Hilda with shock, so she addressed the guards. "My name is Hilda Perry..." she didn't get to finish before the guard came into the cell and grabbed her by her arm, yanking her roughly to the door. She tried to protest and heard June behind her warn otherwise, so she kept quiet and allowed them to march her off down the hall. There were more cells as they walked along, mostly completely quiet with bedraggled women cowering in the shadows. Further along were small cells, no wider than a door that you couldn't see into, with just a small trapdoor waist high. Behind these doors Hilda could hear moaning and sobbing and wild screaming, the noise horrifying. She was stopped suddenly in front of a solid door, and one guard took out a ring of heavy keys and unlocked it, pushing her through into a very bright room. It took her a few moments for her eyes to adjust.

Hilda was shoved hard in her back again, making her trip up some wooden steps. She looked around and was horrified to find herself standing in the docks inside a full courtroom. It was loud with chatter and high energy, making her heart pound with fear. She looked around nervously for any eyes of support and found no one.

"You will turn and face me," the Judge boomed at her, and the courtroom fell silent as she was shoved roughly onto a bench in the corner of the dock. From this vantage point she could not look behind herself and was forced to stare at the Judge, who was looking at her with bored contempt.

"Mary Cooper, you have been accused of theft from your employer. The punishment for theft is seven years in the colonies. How do you plead?"

Hilda tried to stand and was pushed back down "Sir, my name isn't Mary Cooper, you must have the wrong person, sir?" She felt a glimmer of hope that this might all be a mistake. The Judge looked to someone behind Hilda with one eyebrow raised.

"Your Honour," came a man's voice from behind her, "I have the employer."

She saw the Judge nod and there was a rustling of movement from behind her. She tried to turn but the guards kept her still with their presence.

"And what do you say?" the Judge addressed someone.

"Your Honour," came a woman's voice from behind Hilda. It sounded young and not as refined as she was trying to make out. "My name is Hilda Perry." Hilda gasped and tried to turn around.

"Mrs Cooper, one more movement from you and you will be flogged. Do you understand?" the Judge spoke loudly. Hilda began to cry at the absurdity of the situation, and she put her hands over her face. "Carry on Mrs Perry."

"Thank you, your Honour. As I was saying my name is Hilda Perry, and this is one of my house keepers. I have noticed of late she has become slightly deranged, believing she is I, even to the point of making overtures to my husband. The final straw was when I found her stealing my jewellery." The voice let out a fake sob and the Judge was looking at her with sympathy and nodding. "I have done all I can for her, but I feel she has gone too far."

The Judge looked to someone on his left and asked if sending the insane to the colonies was out of practice and the woman behind Hilda interjected. "Your Honour, she is in no way insane. I am just suggesting, well she is a brilliant housekeeper, and I am sure with a strong hand she would be of assistance to anyone in the colonies."

Hilda stood suddenly and swung around to see Moll Myrtle standing in the witness box, dressed in Hilda's clothes, smirking at her. Hilda rose to jump out of the dock, screaming at Moll, before she was grabbed roughly by two soldiers and tightly restrained.

"I have warned you already to control yourself. Mary Cooper, I sentence you to seven years in New South Wales. Guards, take her to the yard for a dozen lashes and see if we can teach her some control." He waved them off with his hand and Hilda's mind snapped. She started screaming her name and her innocence, kicking her legs around to try and get away. It was useless but her will was strong. Hilda was dragged back through the heavy door and down the hall again. She tried scratching the guard's eyes, kicking and thrashing about until she was panting with exhaustion. Eventually she let her body go limp and pleaded quietly to the guards who were now dragging her along the cold stones, but they ignored her. They were looking forward to whipping this feisty wench.

She was taken past the cells and out into the cold yard where she was stripped to the waist and her wrists tied above her head. The humiliation of her exposed body took her mind over the edge, and she slumped against the pole she was tied to and passed out.

6

Angus Drew was starting to get worried. Hilda hadn't returned the day before as she said she would, which wasn't a problem where the Inn was concerned, he could manage by himself during the week. But it was most unlike her to stay away. He knew there must be some issues going on at home, so he just finished out the day and went home to his humble lodgings at the boarding house.

The next morning, he went to the Inn a bit later in the morning, knowing he was up to date with the brewing, and was completely floored to see a For Sale sign in the window. He tried his keys in the locks and found them all to be useless. The building was dark inside, and no smoke came from the chimneys.

Straight away he thought of Hilda. She wouldn't do this without talking to him first. He pulled his coat tighter around himself and headed off towards her house.

He rounded the corner to find her driveway full of horses and carts, coachmen ambling around talking amongst themselves and trying to keep warm. It was then that he saw the carriage that belonged to Eadlin Clarke, Hildas married daughter. He had a sudden sense of foreboding and started towards the house at a run. He passed all the coachmen and went around the back of the house to the servant's entrance and banged loudly on the door. It was opened by the night maid, her face a mess of tears, who sobbed once and then allowed him to embrace her.

"What the devil is going on?" he finally got a chance to ask between her loud sobs. Mrs Dawson waddled down the hall towards them, the same sort of look about her and she pushed the night maid to the side, telling her to keep it together, before embracing Angus herself.

"Oh, Mr Drew," she shook her head and held back a tear. "The worst has happened. Mrs Perry was robbed and murdered yesterday morning. A brutal attack." She held her handkerchief up to her mouth and her eyes became moist. The night maid could be heard sobbing loudly further back in the kitchen. Mrs Dawson led Angus into the warm kitchen by his arm, and he saw several more staff coming in and out the servery door looking forlorn. Eadlin's housekeeper was sitting at the table and rose to embrace Angus.

"Oh Mr Drew, you look so confused. Has no one bothered to tell ye?" She raised a hand up to his face and cupped his cheek. "And you being Hilda's closest friend and all." Angus stood in the middle of the room, absolutely frozen on the spot. The servants moved around him, occasionally giving him a kind glance. "Here, I'll go ask Miss Eadlin if you can go in and say your last goodbyes."

"Are you still having trouble calling her Mrs Clarke?" Mrs Dawson asked her softly. "You'll have to get used to it you know."

"Oh aye, it's a hard thing to change after twenty years, is it not?" Eadlin's housekeeper wandered off through the servery doors, mumbling something about things needing to change all the time, and within moments Eadlin burst through the door and raced to throw her arms around Angus. He held her for a while, her feet barely touching the ground, before he lowered her and let her drag him to the seats at the end of the enormous preparation table.

"Oh Angus, I can't believe no one has told you what is going on," she kept his hand in hers. "I just can't believe it myself. And father insists on a closed coffin, so how are we meant to say our final farewells?" Eadlin started to cry now, and Angus put a big hand on her shoulder.

"Closed coffin, you say. Eadlin, lass, where did this all happen. Do you know?" he spoke gently to keep Eadlin calm.

"Not far from the Inn, that is what I have been told." She was looking at him slightly confused about the question.

"What have the police said about the matter? They must have spoken at length with Mr Perry?" he pushed on and looked up to see Mrs Dawson listening in.

"I don't really know. Father has told me I am not to bother with the details."

Angus looked at Mrs Dawson. "Have you seen the police here at all, Mrs Dawson?" She slowly shook her head and her tears had stopped.

"What is it Angus, what are you suggesting?" Eadlin was completely confused. "I am sorry father is selling the Inn. I know how much you enjoyed working there. It seems quite impetuous that he should bother with such a thing as soon as mother has passed away. I'm not very happy with father's decisions at the moment. He is acting rather cold about this."

Angus stood and kissed Eadlin on the forehead. "I'll be off now, lass."

"Don't you want to go in and say goodbye?" Eadlin asked, surprised.

"I'll say my goodbyes over an ale, I think. Best I be looking for some work. Stay strong, lass, you've a lot of your mother in your character, and it will get you a long way in life." Angus walked out of the kitchen feeling everyone's gaze on his back. Out in the cold he shivered violently, not so much from the weather but more from the shock of what he had just been told. He couldn't stop thinking about how upset Hilda had been on that night. If only she had of told him what was vexing her.

Something felt terribly wrong about this situation, just…off. He walked swiftly back to the Inn and went down the back alley to the staff door. He took his hanky out of his pocket and wrapped it around his knuckles before punching through the glass twice to get his arm in and unlocked the door from the inside. He kicked the heavy door in and crunched over the shattered glass on his way to Hilda's office. Finding a box, he started filling it with all the beer making books, journals and family secrets. Private articles of Hilda's and any cash hidden in the fake bookshelves that Hilda had stashed there to keep it out of William's thieving hands. He then went out to the boiling rooms and filled a large crate with Hilda's late father's coopering tools and thermometers. When he finished, he slowly looked around the room and felt a deep sadness and loss.

He sighed and shook his head, put the box and crate in the wooden wheelbarrow and left through the wide delivery door, purposefully not turning to look back.

7

"Hilda, wake up Hilda," June dabbed gently at Hilda's back with a damp rag. The welts had stopped seeping, and the skin was raised and angry looking. June had watched them earlier drag in Hilda's limp body and throw her to the ground like a rag doll just inside the cell door. She had to hold herself back from running to Hilda until the guards had moved on down the hall. Several of the women had helped June lift Hilda's lifeless form over to the straw bedding, bringing a small pail of water and the cleanest rag they could find. June had prayed that Hilda had passed out before the flogging had begun, her soft scented skin showing she would have never encountered such pain in her life. June dabbed gently a few more times and saw a faint movement in Hilda's body before she heard her groan. "Don't move too fast love," June put a hand to Hilda's shoulder. "You'll make the bleeding start again."

"Where am I?" Hilda whispered and cringed at June's touch.

"Back in the cell, love. They've given you twelve lashes. Did you not keep your head about you as I warned?" June stopped the dabbing and helped Hilda sit up and carefully put her dress back up over her body. They did it slowly, in movements bound by the look of pain on Hilda's face.

"It was her," Hilda looked at June and tears ran down her face. "It was the woman, Moll Myrtle, that I threw out of my house just the night before." Hilda wiped her hand along her face to push away the tears and left a mess of mud and tears across her cheek. "My husband brought home a young woman from The Men's Club, claiming she needed work. I refused out of instinct, but my housekeeper told me of the character of the girl, and later that night I found a letter in my husband's bedside drawer, addressed to my husband, saying he needed a good woman to take care of him." Hilda took a sip of the foul water June was handing her and noticed all the women had come over now to listen to her story. She sat in silence for a while trying to absorb what was happening, her back throbbing with the rough material of her dress chafing the cuts like sand on glass.

"Sounds like you've been had, deary," a woman behind June piped up, and received a stern look from June.

"They did not believe me; the Judge, everyone in the courtroom. As soon as she said I was insane everyone just believed it to be true. There was no one there to speak for me at all, and I just snapped." Hilda started to cry again, and June stopped her.

"Welcome to the other side of life, Hilda Perry. I don't know how easy a life you have had to this point, hopefully not too easy, because this whole new world is going to be harder on you than it will on us." June looked around at the other women. "You see, we are who they say; pick pockets, whores and swindlers. We was just unfortunate enough to get caught." The other women were nodding. "But if there is one thing this life has taught me, Hilda, it's that if you don't put your big girl pants on and toughen up a bit, you won't make it through to the end. And that end for you, deary, should be some sweet revenge." June was smiling an evil smile, and the other women tittered at the thought of some vengeance that they too could live vicariously through.

"Revenge. Yes, I guess that's all I have left," Hilda was nodding. She wiped away the last of her tears with the back of her hand, making a tribal mess on her face, but she didn't give a damn. Her name was Hilda Perry, once the quiet little people pleaser, and look where that had gotten her, rotting in hell. So, she mentally closed the door on that version of herself and imagined looking at a new door in front of her. She pictured lifting her high ankle boot and kicking that door open.

And so started day one of plotting.

* * *

The women were woken roughly in the morning, with a kick and a yell. Forced to get up, they were herded into a washroom and told to scrub themselves clean from the wine barrels of water around the room. The guards gave them no privacy, so the women turned their backs to them; at least they couldn't see the sadism in their eyes. The water had something in it that burned their skin. Anywhere there was an open wound or scab the water burnt like fire. The women shivered through the humiliation and silently wept.

Rough woollen sack like dresses were thrown onto the ground behind them and they were ordered by the leering guards to put them on. They helped each other dress to speed up the process before they were barked at to march out of the washroom. Each woman was given a bundle to carry which contained a blanket and a wooden spoon. They hugged these simple items close to their body, fearing they would never get another. Back through the watchhouse they walked and out a door that led to the outside of the prison. The air was freezing, and their bare feet ached in the snow as they were led towards a towering timber merchant ship which was docked at the wharf. People milled about carrying items, barrels and wood crates and loaded them onto the merchant ship to take to New Holland. The women were pushed roughly up the weather softened gangplank, and their names checked off a list as they boarded. Hilda wanted to tell the man she was not Mary Cooper, but the woman before her had been struck across the head by a soldier for asking a simple question, and the blood oozed slowly from her wound, binding her grey hair. So, Hilda kept quiet. She kept her head down and let her hair fall across her face to hide from the lascivious looks the women received from some of the sailors and Officers.

Quietly she followed the line as they were directed down into their Cradle, the name for the underdeck holding areas for the convicts, a nasty smelling small room that was to sleep twelve of them for the next six months. They were two to a bed, and Hilda felt June grab her arm and drag her as close to the small pot belly fire as was possible for the warmest bunk. In one corner was a cask with drinking water and next to it a bucket for their shared toilet. Light came in through the grate hatch above their bunks, but so did the snow. Eventually a canvas would be put across the grate when it began to rain, but it would just make the small room feel dark and suffocating.

"Oh June, I don't know how I'm going to bear this for six months," Hilda sighed looking around the tiny space and watching the women squeeze themselves onto the beds. "We are nothing more than animals to them."

June was fussing about putting some coal on the small heater. "Oh, you will bear it, Hilda. Its either that or perish." June sat back down on the thin straw mattress and looked Hilda in the eyes. "Not all these women will make it," she whispered and waved her hand about. "I have heard the stories. They will have crammed forty or so women on this privately owned, floating hell. They need to keep as many of us alive as they can to get their money from the Government at the other end. But pay attention Hilda, they don't need to keep all of us alive, that's why they overload us. So, you and I are going to make sure we make it, do you hear me lass?"

Hilda let that sink in and regrouped her thoughts. Yes, there would be no revenge if she failed. She had created a picture in her mind of Moll Myrtle, standing on a pyre and tied to a pole, where Hilda would flick a light and the whole thing would go up in fire. She knew it was wicked, but it made her feel better none the less.

8

"I am Captain Drake, commander of this ship," a tall, weather worn man stood at the bars of their Cradle with his nose in the air, looking at the women as if they were trash, "and I will not tolerate insubordination. Any nonsense will see you flogged and put in irons." He nodded to the soldier standing behind him and walked up the steep steps and out of the hold.

"Man of few words," June sneered to his leaving form and walked a few steps to the bars. "So, what is it going to take for you and me to have an understanding soldier?" she purred as she put her arm through the gap and touched his uniformed chest. He smiled at her and nodded, taking a quick look up the stairs to make sure the captain was gone.

"I believe we can come to some sort of arrangement, m' lady," he said and sat back on his stool with a smug look on his face.

June walked back to the bunk and winked at the other women.

"What was that about?" Hilda whispered.

"That was about keeping us alive, my dear." June sat next to Hilda and laughed at the look on her face. "You've a lot to learn my friend," she said and patted Hilda's knee.

The ship set sail just before midday and the canvas was taken off the grate to let in some much-needed fresh air. Two of the women had already been violently ill from the motion and several others were crying. Hilda sat lost in her own thoughts wondering how long William and his whore had been planning this. It seemed too well thought out for either of them. And what of Angus and her beautiful Inn. What were their plans there? Surely Angus would be wondering by now where she had gone. The wickedness of their actions against her proved they would spend the necessary time concocting lies about her where-abouts to cover their deceit. Hilda fumed at the thought of that horrible little tramp living in her house, touching her things and pretending, to all who didn't know her, that she was Hilda.

But mostly, with her heart, she thought of her daughter Eadlin. What could they possibly have told her that she would believe? Eadlin was too canny to buy just any sort of lie, it would have to be something final. A tear ran down Hildas face; they would have to tell her that her mother was dead. That is the only way they could stop Eadlin looking for her. Oh, the ache in her heart to think that her daughter might think she was deceased. She cupped her mouth to hold in a sob; there could be nothing worse they could do to her daughter. The absolute evilness of them both.

Hilda felt June put an arm around her shoulder and leaned into her and cried. "This is the last time I let you weep, dear Hilda, so let it all out."

Hilda was broken out of her sorrow by a tussle going on at the end of the bunks. There was barely enough room to move about, let alone have a full fight, and June stood to break it up. It got worse before it got better, with hair pulling and screaming, spitting and scratching, and it wasn't long before the head warden strode purposefully down the steps. He motioned for the soldier to open the heavy door and ripped the two fighting women out by their hair. Caught off guard, the women were easily dragged up to the deck and out of sight.

It was hard to make out what was being said above over the sound of the waves against the hull and the moans from the woman hugging the toilet bucket, repeatedly vomiting. Hilda looked up and saw June by the door whispering with the soldier. They spoke for a while, and she came back and sat with Hilda while the soldier went upstairs.

"He'll find out what's going on, Hilda," June said without looking at her. She kept her gaze to the bars and when the soldier came back, she dashed to meet him. They spoke for a while with all the women staring on silently until June came back to the bunk.

"They are both getting fifteen lashes apiece for causing a ruckus, and a night in the irons. The Surgeon is up there to make sure it don't get out of control, but I hear tell he's a drunken fool and will give us no support." June truly looked like she was troubled by the punishment, making Hilda think the two women may have been her friends. "Oh no, I barely know them, Hilda, but to leave them out in the freezing cold for the night tells me our captain has little regard for our wellbeing. We must keep ourselves out of trouble," she looked around at all the women. "All of us, you understand?" The women all nodded together, even the one holding the bucket.

The evening wore on and the sky turned black. The canvas was placed over the grate again and the women were given their night rations to warm up on their small fire. Lumpy porridge and a wedge of hard bread, but for many of the women, it was the first thing they had eaten all day.

The cell now smelt vile, and June asked the soldier if she could empty the bucket. They both left, and were gone for some time, before June was escorted back with something wrapped in a rag. She sat down next to Hilda and motioned for her to raise her dress so June could get to her back. Hilda was confused but did as she was bid, and within moments a soothing salve was gently applied to her aching back. It was cool and warm at the same time and made her feel sleepy.

"Did you do that for me?" she asked June.

"Oh, aye," she whispered, "I'm fairly sure you would do the same for me come the time. Now, shuffle over and I'll show you what I did for me." June opened the rag a little more and produced a small vial of liquid and drank it all in one go.

"Is, is that laudanum?" Hilda naively asked.

"Aye, tis my fall from grace. Now get some sleep Hilda, it's the tiredness can send you mad as well, you know." June snuggled into her one cover and fell instantly asleep, leaving Hilda wide awake and wondering if she could survive this nightmare.

9

On the first morning, Hilda woke with aching muscles and bones from the cramped conditions and the damp coldness of her bunk. June was standing up by the bars talking to the soldier again, so Hilda took the opportunity to stretch out her legs. The ship was sailing flat waters, and the canvas had been removed from the top grate showing a small peak of sunshine.

"Ah, so you're finally awake, are you?" June was leaning over the bunk now looking down at Hilda "Up ya get, old girl, we'll be ordered on deck soon. Time to air out our kits." She dragged Hilda off the bed and took her blanket and the mattress and carried it to the iron bars. Right on cue the warden came down and started yelling at the women to get up. The soldier opened the door and June marched straight out, making sure Hilda was hot on her heels. The warder pushed past the two women and started hitting the bunks with his truncheon. He called the women vile names and threw water on the ones that had not yet woken up. Hilda was mortified by the way he was treating them.

"No," she heard June warn from in front of her. "Don't get involved, they wouldn't do it for you."

Hilda had to look away and followed June up the steps. The bright light of the day hit them at the open door, and they took a second to adjust their eyes. They were pushed to the side of the ship and told to lay their mattress on the railings and beat any bugs out that may be in it. The other women were filing out now and they looked very dishevelled. Hilda looked around her and tried to find the two women that were taken last night.

"They didn't make it Hilda," June said quietly, reading her mind. "Now, turn around and look out at the sea, lest you get a flogging for being nosy."

Hilda turned immediately but it was too late, the captain had seen her and was walking over. He came so close to her she could feel his body touching hers behind her. He bent down to talk in her ear, causing more unwanted contact.

"Mollisher," he whispered venomously, "what are you looking for?" He paused and breathed calmly, "I suggest you keep your shrew eyes to the seas, or I'll have you rump'd." He was leaning in so close his breath moved her hair; she was sure he was smelling her, and she could feel him getting erect. Someone called the captain from further away and he stopped what he was doing and stood back from her. Hilda realised she had been holding her breath and exhaled quietly. She stayed still, hunched over, fearing to even move. She heard his boots on the planks as he walked off, and she heard all the sailors start to speak again.

"Argh Jesus, Hilda, you've gone and got the captain's attention. I fear this will not be an easy journey fer you, my friend." June kept looking out at sea as she spoke, the other women next to them, now hanging their mattresses over the rail, were looking sideways at Hilda with pity. "You'll have to tame your English pride my girl, or it will get flogged out of you."

There was a sudden scream from one of the women and Hilda turned to see her standing on the railing. Her eyes were wild as she hung onto the standing rigging. The wind blew back her knotted hair and she howled like a wolf and threw herself over the edge. The men who had run to stop her were too late, and they all watched her hit the waves hard and roll under the hull.

"Do not move a muscle," Hilda heard June say from next to her. There was shouting about the deck and a woman on Hilda's other side let out a sob. She felt the captain behind her again, and she froze.

"Take the wretches back inside," he said calmly and put a hand on Hilda's shoulder. "Send this one to my cabin and have her scrub every inch of it." He took his hand off her shoulder and walked away.

Hilda felt sick to the stomach and could feel June staring at her. A warden grabbed her arm roughly and walked her in the opposite direction to all the other women. She told herself she wouldn't cry and lifted her chin in the air, ignoring all the lewd noises the sailors were making. She thought of June, and then William. His whore and his mother. She thought of Eadlin and nearly lost her composure. So, she settled her mind on Angus and straightened her back.

The captain's cabin was spacious and light, from the windows behind his great desk, which was littered with paper and rolls, compasses and quills. A flagon of wine sat half full on the desk with a golden goblet, that had fallen on its side and rolled casually back and forward with the ship's movement. A sheet was used as a partition for the sleeping bunk, and a table and two chairs took up another corner. The warden came back in and roughly handed her a wooden bucket with a scrubbing brush and a square of soap floating in the top, and it slushed over, wetting her sack dress before he left.

Hilda felt relief that perhaps she was only required to clean the cabin and exhaled a long breath. But it was too soon, and she heard the door behind her open and then close.

"What are you waiting for?" the captain snapped behind her, "Clean." He walked around her still body and took a seat at his desk. Hilda risked a quick look at him and was confused to see he was writing in a journal and wasn't watching her at all. So, she started to clean.

The captain came and went while she cleaned and did not address her again until she had finished. She stood in front of his desk, with her head bowed, holding the handle of the bucket. He felt her stillness and stood up, and walking over to her he stood, too close.

"Are you done?" he said, and she nodded. He didn't say anything for a few seconds and Hilda refused to raise her eyes and look at him.

She could see his chest rise and fall as he breathed, and she felt his hand go to her hair, and then stop just before he touched it.

"Soldier!" he yelled over her making her jump, and the door behind her opened. "Take her away," he said calmly. Hilda was grabbed by her arm and pulled back out the door, and she didn't raise her head until the door was closed behind them.

The soldier didn't talk to her; he just pushed her along by shoving her in the back. She threw the dirty water over the rail and left the bucket with the others. The sailors all looked at her when she passed them, and she kept her chin high and ignored their suggestive remarks. She was pushed down the steps to the women's cradle and jammed through the iron bar door. All the women were quiet and staring at her.

"Are you alright, Hilda?" June stood and embraced her.

"He didn't touch me," Hilda said loud enough for them all to hear and there was a collective sigh of relief. "I had to clean his cabin and then he sent me away. It was very strange."

June stood back and looked at her friend confused. "Not even once?" she asked slowly and watched as Hilda shook her head.

"Don't get comfortable wench," the sailor jibed from his stool. "I expect you'll start to look better as the journey goes on." The soldier laughed at his joke as he stuffed tobacco in a pipe.

10

The days rolled into weeks on the ship and the weather started to get hotter. The occasional violent storm had made for uncomfortable sailing, with one storm so bad the animal's waste from the cargo area had washed through the hatches and putrefied the men's and women's holding cradles. The ship was smashed about for another hour before the convicts could be brought out of the holds and made to scrub out the area with gunpowder. But they had spent too long in the filth, and several of the women in Hilda's cradle now had fever, and wracking coughs came from their chests. Their clothes were filthy, and what water was left was now rationed.

It was too hot now to light the little stove, so they ate their rations cold and lumpy.

The women heard talk that the male convicts had tried a mutiny and a whole day was put aside for their floggings. One hundred each for their troubles and three hundred for the ring leaders. The hatches were all opened so the other convicts could hear the agony of the punishment, and five of the men didn't survive the brutal lashings.

Hilda had been called on several more occasions to go to the captain's cabin and clean it. And each time he had acted the same, but after the animal faeces spill, she had smelt putrid and having no other clothes to change into she wasn't called on again. However, she felt his presence when she came on deck and his eyes on her every move. June had no idea what the man was playing at and feared for her friend.

On a calm hot day, the ship berthed in Rio De Janeiro and all the sailors were allowed leave to go ashore. The soldiers and warders were made to stay on board and bring all the convicts onto the deck to be sorted according to their physical and mental health. The ship's doctor moved among the wretched mob, drunk and useless. He chose several of the emaciated children and women and wrote their names in his journal and moved them to one side in a vain attempt to treat their many woes.

Hilda and June sat together as always, looking just as thin and wild as the rest of them. The sun was hotter than they had ever felt it, and the sweat ran down their already filthy bodies adding to the smell.

One rowboat came back to the ship laden with sacks containing fresh clothes and soap and they were all ordered to fill the buckets with sea water and wash themselves. There was little privacy between the men and women, and the sun was searing as they scrubbed themselves raw and changed their clothes. Ordered to throw all the old garments over the side, they were given fruit and cured meat to fill their stomachs.

"It's like Christmas, June," Hilda spoke between mouthfuls. "I almost feel human again."

"This is not for your benefit my friend. Look around, the captain has lost too many of us. If he isn't careful, he won't get the Government money owed him, come the colony." June was full of spite for the captain. "The Surgeon Superintendent will inspect the ship on arrival and if we are in poor condition, he'll not be paid a penny."

They watched as their bedding was thrown over the side and new straw and covers shoved at them to make new mattresses.

"I don't care the reason, June. I'll take what little comfort I'm afforded at this point." Hilda stuffed the straw June was passing her into the cover and snuck a quick look around the ship. Her timing was off again, and she found herself staring straight into the eyes of the captain as he stood behind the wheel. She couldn't drag her gaze away quick enough and cursed herself for her stupidity once again. Had he watched her dress? How long had he stood there?

As the sun was setting, they were forced back into the cells where they sat and listened to the whooping cries of the returning drunken sailors. Their guard had left for his shore leave, and the women realised they were now defenceless against the drunk sailor's advances, and they cowered in the corner and kept quiet.

"I swear if they come down here, I'll kill them," one of the women whispered, and several agreed.

Nevertheless, the heavy wood door above the steps was opened and the women heard footsteps coming down. The sailors were laughing and leering and reeked of rum and tobacco. One of them held the ring of keys to the door and struggled to get a key in the lock, staggering around until he dropped the ring. The other sailors tried to pick them up, but they were too inebriated and fell over each other with the effort. The women pushed back against each other even tighter into the corner.

"Out, you dogs," the captain's voice could be heard at the top of the steps, although the women couldn't see him. "Go sleep it off." The women watched as the sailors skulked off and waited until they heard the door slam shut before breathing a collective sigh of relief.

"It seems your relationship with the captain may benefit us after all," one of the women spoke to Hilda as they crawled back into their bunks.

11

Angus sat at the end of the bar slowly and purposefully getting drunk. He spent his days now coopering ale for The Red Lion Inn, a slightly more upmarket place than he was used to, who had commandeered his immeasurable talents of brewing as soon as they had found out he was out of work. The owners put up with the fact that he was in a constant state of misery and particularly hard to work with, in exchange for the perfect ale that he produced which had doubled their clientele. His appearance was dishevelled, and his beard was long with a salt and pepper look to it. He was a little thin for his height and his broad square shoulders seemed a little bony and hunched over now. Nobody knew of what was bothering him, they just assumed that was his demeaner and left him to it.

The end of the day, Angus was allowed the furthest seat from the paying clientele and given a bottomless cup of rum until he either fell off the stool or staggered upstairs to his room mumbling about the injustices of life. Cook always put a plate of food in front of him but he rarely touched it.

On his day off he would walk to the other side of town and stand outside Hilda's Inn, reopened now but attracting a much lower class of people, with cheap ale and watered down rum. It had been near on six months now since he had lost Hilda, and he still to this day could not believe she had died. It just didn't feel right, something was not making sense.

William and his homewrecker had settled into their new life quite easily, according to Mrs Dawson, who had been fired along with the other staff and replaced immediately with people of Moll Myrtle's choosing. Hilda's grand house had been re-washed and re-gardened and now looked like a tacky whorehouse, as Mrs Dawson referred to it. There was even preparation under way for a lavish wedding. Mrs Dawson told Angus that she believed, as soon as the two were wed, Moll would probably have Mr Perry done away with. Mrs Dawson had been fairly drunk by this stage of the conversation, so Angus wasn't sure about that one. He thought it wouldn't be such a bad thing; he would have liked to do it himself most days. Time had moved on swiftly and people had just gone on with their lives as if Hilda had never existed. But Angus couldn't get past it. He had told Hilda's father he would never let anything happen to her. He had failed.

Angus looked deep into his cup and whispered to his rum that he had failed.

He felt someone close to his elbow and lifted his head and tried to look sober; it was Eadlin. He immediately jumped off his stool and wrapped his arms about her, lifting her off the ground.

"Oh Eadlin, dear child, you are a sight for sore eyes," he was teary and slurring his words.

Eadlin laughed at him and hit him on the arm.

"Put me down, you big brute, you stink of rum." He lowered her, still laughing, and looked to the ground in embarrassment. "Come now, Angus, this is no good. Look at you," she said as she touched his long-matted hair with a grimace and grabbed at his beard. "There is nothing for it, you are coming with me." She took hold of his large hand and turned to leave the Inn, surprised to find everyone staring and wondering what such a well-dressed young woman was doing with the beast from the end of the bar. Just like her mother, she stuck her chin up, and without letting go of Angus's hand, marched out of the building.

Out on the busy street, Eadlin had to keep hold of Angus's hand and arm to keep him on the footpath and off the road. Every time she looked up at him, she saw he was staring down at her with a goofy grin on his face, and she would shake her head and laugh.

"I've spoken with your employer, Angus, and he has agreed to let you have the evening off." She smiled up at him again. "However, I did have to promise him I would get you cleaned up and more presentable." Eadlin stopped short in front of the barber's door causing Angus to run into the red and white striped pole. She laughed and spun him around, pushing him through the door and onto a chair.

"Good evening, sir," she addressed the barber, who was looking up and down at Angus as if he were a homeless person. "We would like the works. But don't shave the beard completely off, when trimmed it makes my friend here look very distinguished." She smiled down at Angus and laughed. "Well, that is what mother used to always say." She winked at Angus, and he smiled broadly "I'm off to get you some new clothes for your new adventure, I won't be long." Eadlin left the barbers like a woman on a mission.

"New adventure?" Angus said aloud, "What the devil does that mean?"

The barber pushed Angus's head back onto the head rest and lay a steamy warm towel across his chin, making him relax enough to close his eyes.

12

Angus sat in the King Street tearooms feeling a little out of place surrounded by such well to do ladies all talking at the same time, or so it seemed to his ears.

"Focus now, Angus," Eadlin bought him back to the present and the lady's hat which sat in front of him on the table. "What do you see here?" she pointed to the hat with a determined look on her face, and he was completely unsure of what she wanted him to say, so he looked up at her with a blank expression.

"It appears to be a lady's hat?" he trailed off at the end due to her look of annoyance.

"Look closer, Angus," she snapped at him and then apologised at the wounded look on his face. "This isn't just any lady's hat. Look at the feather on the side here." She touched the feather gently and had a sad look on her face, "What is the feather of Angus?'

"Well, it looks like a pigeon feather," he smiled at a memory "Not unlike the one I put in your mother's hat the day we had to chase a pigeon out of the rafters." He chuckled at the thought and then looked at Eadlin in surprise. She was nodding, finally thankful he had caught on. "Is this Hilda's hat, child?" He instantly picked it up and turned it over, feeling under the leather band until his fingers touched the lucky note Hilda's father had put in the rim. He looked at Eadlin again, confused.

"Last night I had a visitor to my house. I didn't get to see who it was because the cleaner answered the door." Eadlin sat forward and took one of Angus's large hands in both of hers. "The visitor left this hat with a note for me saying that mother wasn't dead at all, and that if I wanted to find her, I would have to pay." Eadlin was loving the look on Angus's face, a mixture of joy and concern, anger and relief.

"I don't like the idea of someone coming to your house, lass," he interjected.

"Oh, for goodness' sake, Angus, stay with me on this," she shook her head and laughed at him like he was a schoolboy. "I know you feel, as I do, that there can be no way mother is dead. It's simply unfeasible. She wouldn't have allowed it," and they both laughed at this.

"Are we clutching at straws because we want her back?" Angus asked, touching the hat trying to hide his feelings.

"Maybe we are and maybe we aren't. But I need to know more, and I know you do too."

Angus looked at the paper wrapped package sitting on the floor, which Eadlin had brought in with them. "I have a feeling you have a plan lass, and the look of mischief on your face right now has me nervous about it."

Eadlin was struggling to hide her excitement as she pulled the note out of her purse and handed it to Angus to read. "There is an address there of where to meet this person and hand over the money in exchange for mother's whereabouts, and it's down at the port. I don't think he knows that since father took in that shrew, I no longer receive my annual salary and don't have that sort of money. So, my thinking is..." she paused for effect and Angus put his head in his hand to massage his temple. This was going to hurt, "...I have brought some wharfie clothes for you here," she pointed at the bag on the floor, "And I want you to follow me to the meeting point and we can get a jump on this scamp and find out what we need to, then dump him in the river."

Angus looked up at Eadlin and shook his head slowly. "That is *not* a good idea." He tried not to laugh at the sulky look on her face, "When did you decide to become a mollisher, my girl?"

"Well, there is a plan B," she said with a sulk, and he laughed and motioned for her to carry on. "I do know where the safe is at fathers.

If we can find a safe cracker, I am sure there are plenty of notes in there to fund our needs." Eadlin was happy to see Angus nodding at this idea and smirked to herself at the knowledge he would go along with any plan to upset her father.

"Now you're making sense. We need to get in there while they are out, and you can distract the servants while I open the safe."

Eadlin was smiling at Angus with one eyebrow raised. "Can you crack a safe then?"

"Oh aye, I wasn't always the fine gentleman you see before you now," Angus laughed and read the note again. "We've got three days to plan this before the meet up, best we get cracking then."

They left the tea rooms on somewhat of a high, discussing their plans down to finer details. Finding out if Hilda was still alive was the most exciting part, messing with Eadlin's father was just a bonus. Eadlin left Angus at the door of the Red Lion Inn and planted a kiss on his cheek. He walked into the bar and watched the barman fill his cup with rum, so he put his hand up to refuse the drink. As he walked up the steps to his room, he had to laugh at overhearing the confused chatter from the barmen in his wake.

13

Hilda and June stood by the bars of the cradle and listened intently to the voices up the stairs. It was so hot the sweat ran down their backs freely, and they had to keep wiping their eyes to keep out the stinging drops that ran down from their brows. The ship had been sitting idle in Sydney Cove for a full night and day now, waiting for the Surgeon Superintendent and the Principal Superintendent of Convicts to come out and inspect the prisoners.

Hilda turned and looked at the sad state of the women that had survived the six-month trip. Of the original twelve in this cradle, they had lost five. The two women that had fought at the start of the trip and had been flogged and left on deck in irons to freeze, and two more to sickness and the one who had gone mad and thrown herself overboard. That was just in this cradle, Hilda and June had heard rumours from the soldier June attended, that much the same had occurred in the other cradles. This would not bode well for the captain, and he took his temper out on the sailors at every chance he had.

Some of the women were marked with sores that oozed a pus that never healed, and some of the women had lost great chunks of hair from the stress. The soldier who June had been attending to, Mr Day, had told them that it was usual to take the female convicts to a hospital and make them well again before they were assigned as servants. The sailor had shown a paper to Hilda and June which read;

'Settlers and inhabitants who wish to procure a female servant, upon the arrival of a vessel with prisoners, are required to send in their applications to the secretary's office next week. It is understood that each settler will be required to engage for the maintenance of the servant, which may be assigned, for 12 months, unless declared to be discharged by the sentence of a Magistrate. By Command of His Honour H.E Robinson Sec.'

"I'm going to apply for you June," Mr Day had said, looking at her with puppy dog eyes. "I'm done soldiering, I want a farm and a family."

June had scoffed playfully in his face, "I will not be doing farmwork. Getting all dirty with a bent back and wrinkles from the hot sun," but she had told Hilda her plan with this man months ago. Better to be with a kind man that she could control than a domineering, merciless swine. It was June that had planted the seed of him leaving the corps and taking up farming. Why, a retired soldier was practically given a plot of land for free in New South Wales, to farm and keep the continent in food supplies.

"I'd never make you work in the sun, June," he had said, "It would ruin your beautiful white skin."

June knew she had him where she wanted him, even writing the application for him to hand in to the secretary's office. He was far from a pleasant or handsome looking man, but he was gentle in his love making and attentive in his treatment of June, and that's all she needed to get through her seven years.

Footsteps were heard coming down the stairs and the women stepped back to allow in the two finely dressed gentlemen who stood waiting for the soldier to open the cage. They held their hankies to their noses and spoke to each other quietly, before ordering the soldier to bring the ladies up to the deck instead and quickly marched off.

Up on the deck, Hilda tilted her head back and let the salty cool air brush over her face. She looked to the land and felt a strange feeling of dread. The captain had his back to them and was talking animatedly to the two officers from the colony. They were arguing about something, and the captain threw his arms in the air in frustration and ran his hand through his hair. He turned suddenly and Hilda dropped her gaze to the floor.

The women were huddled together, then herded towards the small boats tied to the hulk. Some of the ladies barely had the strength to go down the ladder so they had to support one another. The small boats sat twenty people and there were five boats in total, the last being designated, by the ship's doctor, to the near dead and violently ill. The sailors rowed them ashore in silence, enjoying the breeze on their skin. Ahead, soldiers stood in wait of the boats, looking hot, but crisp and clean, in their red wool coat jackets, white trousers and button up gaiters over their boots.

The women had been told of the hierarchy of the new colony, starting from the Kings delegates and magistrates, officers and colonials that had come over to make a new life. Then there were the free convicts, who had done out their time and could not afford, or in some instances didn't want to go back to England. There was plenty of work around as labourers or farm hands, but even though they were finally emancipated and free, they would forever have the social stigma of being an ex-convict. And lastly, were the convicts. Lower on the social chain than the swine and donkeys.

On the hot sand of the beach the women were pushed and shoved about until there were three groups in all. The women who were the healthiest, the women who could be recovered and the poor wretched souls who would not be long for this world.

There was some shouting from the end group as, yet another old woman dropped to the ground in the heat and passed away. Hilda thought to herself at the sight of her, how unnecessary the death over a stolen loaf of bread and remembered the look on the magistrate's face who had sentenced herself just six months past. It didn't matter at all the circumstances leading to the women being before the courts. There was no chance to explain your situation, plea for leniency, ask for proof of allegations. Everyone was just assumed guilty without a chance to prove their innocence. Hilda understood now what this world was about and knew that to survive this nightmare, she would have to keep her mouth shut and her ears and eyes wide open. To trust no one, lest she lose her chance to sail back to England and enact her revenge, for it was the thought of that revenge that kept the fire burning in her soul, her reason to wake every morning and take care of herself, both mentally and physically. Slowly she was building a steel wall around her heart and a sharp wit about her thoughts. Moll Myrtle would be a fool to think this was over. Moll Myrtle was going to rue the day she messed with Hilda Perry. Moll was nothing more than a nickey vamp, who had only got one over Hilda by taking her by surprise. She had used her body as a lure on Hilda's weak-minded husband and turned him against Hilda with her sex. But where she had gone wrong was employing thugs to carry out her evil plan. Hilda had grown up in the Inn life, and knew firsthand that any lushington looking for a ha'pence would turn on you at the offer of a pound. Hilda smiled to herself and brought her thoughts back to the present.

"I don't know what's on your mind right now, my friend," June whispered out the side of her mouth over Hilda's shoulder, "But I fear for the whelp it's directed at." They both sniggered and stopped immediately at a soldier walking over.

"Get in line, wenches," he said and pushed them in behind the other women. "The Governor has no time for pebble mollishers, and you'll find yourselves slang'd in the square with rotten fruit thrown at ye." He pushed them roughly one more time so that they tripped into the women in front of them. Hilda straightened her shoulders and turned towards the soldier, stopping only by being pinched on the arm by June, who was looking at her and shaking her head.

Hilda looked about herself as she walked and noticed the large British flags fluttering in the breeze above most of the white-washed buildings. Horse drawn carts carrying barrels and bags, ties of wheat and corn, rumbled along the hard rocky tracks that snaked through the settlement. Soldiers walking in pairs and well-dressed women, with parasols to keep out the sun, walked proudly next to their well-dressed, landed gentry partners. Men rode past on single horses, their slops consisting mostly of striped cotton shirts, canvas duck trousers and grey woollen jackets. Caps of kangaroo skins or cabbage tree hats adorned their heads, nodding to the more simply dressed ladies in their plain dresses and aprons with bonnets and caps over their hair.

Hilda was shocked how busy the streets were, with plenty of establishments selling materials for building a home, farming and clothes. She wasn't sure what she had pictured the colonies would be like. She had always thought of it as a dry, arid land full of prisons and starving people. But here in Sydney Cove it was quite lush with tall trees surrounding the settlement, green grass to the white, white sand of the water's edge. The sky was bluer than she had ever seen, a sky with birds of all sizes floating in the gentle, salty breeze.

The first two groups were led to a long building behind the settlement and ushered into a room full of beds made with crisp clean linen and blankets. A matron stood at the door with two nurses and inspected the women one by one before sending them off to the washrooms, where the air smelt clean and the wash tubs were surrounded by privacy screens. Each was handed a slither of soap with an enchanting smell, that Hilda was told was Eucalyptus, to aid in the healing of any sores, and a bundle of crisp clothing. The water was warm and soothing on Hilda's tense body, and she winced slightly as she lowered herself into its depth feeling it caress her dry skin. A nurse came in when Hilda was finished, and she was told to kneel next to her tub and put her head over the water. The nurse poured a liquid into Hilda's hair that burnt her scalp, and she looked to the water below and saw tiny mites falling from her hair into the water. The nurse then rubbed Hilda's soap through her hair roughly and scrubbed Hilda's scalp with her strong fingers. A fresh bucket of water was dumped over her hair and then a towel wrapped it tight, before she could stand and relieve the ache in her back. The nurse didn't speak but handed her a brush, and she was pointed to leave the washroom to dress in the next room with the other ladies.

The matron came in while they were dressing and inspected everyone's sores and cuts, telling the nurses the treatment that was required for each while another nurse took notes in a book. The matron stopped behind Hilda and inspected the lash marks with her finger while making a tutting sound with her mouth.

"Look at the mess of this," she said to one of the nurses. "She'll have these scars for the rest of her days, I fear." She spun Hilda around and looked in her mouth and behind her ears and frowned.

"What is your name?" the matron asked Hilda, looking confused.

"My name is Hilda Perry," Hilda said calmly.

The matron grabbed the name list off the nurse and ran her finger down it. "There is no Hilda Perry on this list?" She looked back to Hilda and roughly opened her mouth again and inspected her teeth. She was just about to say something to Hilda when she was interrupted by the arrival of the Superintendent of Convicts.

"Matron," he tipped his hat to her "Gather up twenty of the strongest women, they are needed down at The Paddock."

"I'll be lucky to find five in decent shape with this new lot," the Matron complained. "What a mess." She shook her head and clucked over the names list.

"Word is the captain's going to be court marshalled this time," he said looking Hilda up and down like she was a cow.

"Oh aye?" she looked up and raised her eyebrow at him. "Nothing ever comes of it, I fear." She told the nurse to gather the women together and strode off down the hallway with the Superintendent in tow.

Hilda looked at the nurse and asked her what The Paddock was. She was told it was a female factory, where women were designated tasks such as cleaning and dressmaking for the free settlers. It was where they worked and slept in Hobart Town. A place where they normally only sent the difficult ladies. She said it was a wretched water crossing to the island and the work was backbreaking, and there had been a fire not a month back in the boiler room where twenty wretched souls had perished. The nurse looked genuinely sad about it as she handed Hilda a shawl and bonnet and guided the ladies through to the reading room.

14

Eadlin kept up the chatter with her father's house staff, whilst looking over their heads at the clock on the wall. She had decided to keep the conversation strategically focussed on gossip, knowing full well that is what would keep the staff in close attention. Occasionally she had to bend the story a little when it looked like they were losing interest, and she prayed she wouldn't go to hell for such falsities. Her mother would be terribly disappointed in her for spreading such malice, but Eadlin kept on, telling herself it was of the utmost importance to give Angus all the time he needed to calmly crack the safe.

William and the shrew were having lunch at the restaurant in town. She had made sure of that by asking the owner, a dear friend of hers, to pretend they had won a complimentary meal for being such special guests. Eadlin knew her father was a penny pincher and would jump at the chance of a free meal and to walk around a fancy restaurant with a much younger woman, making the genteel jealous, or so he assumed. Most people in town thought they looked desperate and ridiculous together.

Angus was upstairs in the office, having gotten the safe open quickly, and he was reading through the paperwork that he had found inside and shaking his head. The sale of the Inn had netted William a tidy sum indeed and the deeds to Hilda's house was now in Moll Myrtle's name only. The bloody fool, Angus thought to himself. Was William's ego so engorged that he could not see what was happening, blind Freddy could have seen. Angus sighed again realising poor old William was not long for this world. He reached in and took all the notes. He was not going to take it all, but he realised now who was intending on ending up with it, so he figured he was doing it for Eadlin. He found a picture of Hilda under all the paperwork and slid it into his shirt pocket, before closing the safe and locking it again. He looked around the office and saw paintings of Moll on the walls, all touched up to make it look like she had no impurities. One of her standing behind William, who sat at his desk looking like a lord, made Angus laugh to himself. The usual warmth and sophistication of Hilda's house was gone, replaced with ruffles and fluff and bad taste in décor. If Hilda was still alive somewhere and he could find her, he doubted she would ever want her home back. It felt different now, the energy of the room was gone.

Angus left the room with a feeling of closure and stole his way down the long hall to the staircase and out the front door. He rang the doorbell on his way out as the agreed signal to Eadlin that he was done and gone, before diving through the hedge that surrounded the house. The plan was to meet Eadlin back at the Red Lion Inn, dress in the wharfie clothes that she had brought him and await her arrival.

He was two rums in when Eadlin entered the Inn and was happy to see her smiling face. She shimmied up onto a bar stool next to him and ordered herself a brandy. They both sipped at their drinks feeling very clever, and waiting until the barman had moved on.

"Are we ready for this evening?" she asked Angus straight away with a touch of excitement in her hushed tone. She looked him up and down and nodded her approval at his attire. "You certainly look the part."

He straightened his collar and ran his hands down his legs. "Been a while since I had new slops," he smiled, "Actually feels quite good."

"Stay focussed, Angus," she said without looking at him and nodded to the barman for two refills. She watched him fill the cups and walk away. "So, you are to follow me to the docks at an agreeable distance for my own safety." She touched the rough wool dress she had put on to make sure she didn't stand out and cleared her throat to keep whispering.

"Eadlin, lass," he stopped her. "We have been through this enough times. I will have my eye on you the whole time, I promise naught will happen to you." He chuckled to himself at the look on her face from being interrupted.

After a while her face relaxed and she smiled. "I do apologise, Angus, I am a little out of my depth here."

Angus finished his rum and double checked the notes were in his breast pocket, before holding out his hand to help Eadlin down off the stool. They left the Inn to the usual curious stares and went down the main street towards the port.

The closer they got to the port, the darker and rougher the streets looked. There were bit-fakers and harlots lurking in the shadows, highwaymen and scamps watching them walk through the streets.

"You go on ahead now," Angus whispered to Eadlin. "Watch out for the little kincher thieves, they'll come upon you all innocent like and steal your shoes if you're not careful." He nodded to her that it was going to be okay and gave her a gentle shove forward.

Eadlin took a handful of steps and turned, to see Angus out of sight. From the shadows behind her he whispered that he was still there, and she gave a sigh of relief and kept on her way. Outside the corner Inns, men were fighting, and women were scantily clad, smiling at Eadlin as she passed, telling her these were their corners, and she should move her business to another. She kept walking and stumbling along until she came to a messy little eatery known as The Greasy Spoon. It was full of customers both sitting and standing, all speaking loudly to hear one another. The smell coming from the building was of old fat and burnt onions, cigarette smoke and unwashed bodies.

Eadlin breathed in and out a few times and steadied herself to go in. She took a quick look behind herself but still couldn't see Angus anywhere and prayed she would make it out of here alive. The plan was to lure the Sharp out of the eatery by telling him the money was with her sister outside. She would show him one of the notes to get his trust, before bringing him out into the open so Angus could get a grab on him. It was too dangerous to do inside, surrounded by this crowd of people. Angus would have ended up with a knife in his back and never seen again, lest they drag the port. Then they were to take him to an empty warehouse that Angus had found and get every bit of information out of the swine that they could. Eadlin had insisted they give the man some money, nowhere near what he was asking but something, after all, he knew where she lived. But most importantly for Angus, he had to know this man was telling the truth. He liked to look a man dead in the eye to tell if he was lying or not.

Eadlin took a couple more breaths, stuck her chin up and pushed her way through. It was so tight inside it was body to body, making her skin crawl, but she pushed her way through the crowd anyway. In the far back corner was a man dressed in a worn woollen suit with a flat cap on his head. He was looking out the grimy window with a cup in his hand. He looked to be in his sixties, which surprised Eadlin, she was expecting to see a younger roughie. He must have sensed her staring and slowly turned his head. His face was weathered from a hard life and his eyes were sad with disappointment.

"Mr Brown, I assume?" Eadlin said too quietly, and was forced to repeat herself. He nodded his head and pointed towards the empty seat in front of him. The crowd was getting louder and there was some pushing and shoving going on in the middle, when a policeman's whistle cut through the noise. The crowd turned frantic, yelling it was the bobbies, until there was mayhem. People were scampering over each other in a free for all and Eadlin could see Angus barging through a side door, shoving people out of the way and calling Eadlin's name. She turned back to the old man and saw that he had gone, and was crushed. She felt her arm grabbed and turned to see Angus, before he threw her over his shoulder and pushed and punched his way back out of the crowd. He put her to her feet outside and grabbed her hand, dragging and stumbling back through the winding streets and out of the area.

"Oh Angus, can we stop now please?" she begged and pulled her hand from his, bending at the waist to get a breath. Angus stopped and breathed heavy, looking around them for any sign of trouble. "What on earth happened back there?"

Angus stopped and looked at her, feeling her disappointment. They were so close. She started to cry, looking into his eyes until it became huge sobs of frustration. Angus gathered her in his arms and patted her shoulder.

"We were so close, lass, I feel what you're feeling now too." He let her cry on for a while until he felt her body go still and her breathing calmer. "I don't know what the hell happened back there; I think we were just in the wrong place at the wrong time." He looked down to see her staring back up at him and nodding, the look in her eyes broke his heart. "We'll get another chance, lass, we're not giving up that easy. Come on, let's get you home."

15

In Hobart Town, Hilda stood with the group of twenty wretched looking women and stared up at the enormous arched sign across the two pillared entrance drive. *Cascades Female Factory* read the roughly etched piece of timber, careless in design as were the cold buildings that stood within. The women were told on the freezing journey across the Bass Straight, the body of water separating the Island state of Tasmania from the mainland, that the Female Factory was once a distillery built by Mr Thomas Yardley- Lowes who was allocated the land near the south harbour by Governor Sorell. But Mr Thomas had been besieged by a series of unfortunate events over the years, and had he opened it when he'd desired, he would have had the only distillery in Van Diemen's Land. Oh, the money that would have made him. But by the time he got it up and running, there were sixteen other establishments going thanks to the reduced import taxes on spirits allowing others to start their own business, and he'd all but done his dough by then. The sailor had laughed at that point in his story and shook his head.

The women wrapped their shawls around themselves tighter to ward off the cold wind that raced down the snowy mountain behind the factory. It was a bitter day, all grey cloud and hovering mist. They sniffled and coughed as they watched a group of six walk towards them. The woman in the crisp white, floor length dress stopped in front of them and made her back stiff.

"Ladies," she addressed them with a curt nod, "Please follow us." Turning on her heel she moved behind the other five official looking people and headed towards the first large building that resembled somewhat a town hall or school room. The women followed woefully, keen to be out of the drizzle, no matter what came next.

The room did in fact have a fire going, and the interior appeared to be a makeshift church. Ordered to stay standing, the Superintendent mounted the rostrum and began his oration after first clearing his throat.

"Ladies," he allowed, "this House of Correction is normally reserved for, and intended to be, equally subserviate to the checking of the growing depravity of the free female population, and of course the fair disobedient amongst the convict populate, awarded its accommodation as a recess to their wild and disorderly propensities. Instead of idleness and sloth, more industrious occupations can occur, such as wool-combing, spinning, with additional amusement of hemp-picking, which have in turn superseded former occupations of tossing each other in blankets and delivering love letters…" {1} The Superintendent trailed off his bloviate rant at a side glace from the Matron. He cleared his throat again and continued.

"In short, the Matron will explain the new regulations for the House of Corrections and how it is managed. All regulations are to be adhered to. Any gross health or fiery temperaments, or any disobedience of any kind for that matter, will see you put in a dark cell until your conduct has been brought under consideration by myself." He nodded curtly and scurried off the rostrum and out of the way of the Matron's oncoming form.

Hilda looked to the other women and was surprised they were all looking at her perplexed. They all knew she was the only one that had had any sort of proper schooling, and assumed she might know what the man had been on about. She had a rough idea but couldn't put it into words quick enough, so she just shrugged her shoulders and played dumb.

"SIT!" The Matron bellowed at the ladies and waited for the scuffling to quiet down. "There is a strict class system enforced here, managed by me, the overseer," the matron pointed to the men and women standing to her left looking like they enjoyed every aspect of their jobs, "the Task Mistress, Porter, Clerk and these two constables." She put her hands on her squashed in hips and eyed all the women individually.

"There are three distinct classes and on no account are they to communicate with one another." She held up her hand and pointed a finger into the air. "Class one; new from England, well behaved and the only class who will be considered for assignment and sent to service when the appropriate employment can be found." She put her hand down and pointed at the women. "This is you, however, due to an incident recently we are in need of cooks, task overseers and hospital attendants which is what your positions will be for the foreseeable future until such time you are replaced." She held her hand up in the air again with two fingers raised.

"Class two; women who have committed minor crimes and are improving their conduct. These women's tasks include the making of clothes for the establishment and mending for the free community. These women can have the opportunity to be promoted to class one." She stuck her third finger in the air and looked at the other officials exchanging knowing glances.

"Class three," she laughed aloud. "Class three include the women who have been transported for the second time, for misconduct on the journey, offences within the walls of the establishment and unsolicited pregnancies." The Matron was nodding and smiling as though she had seen some rough ones in her time. "Class three are designated to the washtubs, orphan school and penitentiary duties, the likes of which you will not want to experience yourself so watch what you do. Class three will never make it out of class three until the end of their sentence or their death, whichever comes the fastest." The other officials sniggered at her joke.

Hilda heard snoring from behind her in the silence that followed the Matron's speech and turned to see the woman behind her had nodded off. Hilda didn't blame her; the lack of sleep and food had worn all the ladies into exhaustion and now sitting in this slightly warm building was the final straw. A bucket of ice-cold water was thrown at the woman, careless of whoever else wore it, and she shrieked awake and proceeded to sit there shivering and alert like a field mouse.

The Matron nodded at the overseer for throwing the water and pursed her lips, slowly eyeing all the women. She didn't bother to say anything else. The bucket of icy water was proof enough to the women that this was not going to be an easy stay. The Matron signalled to the Task Mistress and Porter to move the ladies to their sleeping quarters and exited the building through another door, followed close behind by the Superintendent and Constables. It was obvious to Hilda who ran the factory, and she made a mental note to stay out of the Matron's way.

Back out in the cold the women walked quickly through the courtyard and eyed the old buildings with small windows. Over one wall that was topped with broken glass they could hear children moving about and talking to one another, which Hilda accepted must be the orphanage. She had been told the women who were brought here saw out their pregnancies and were made to wean the child in just nine months, which the midwives believed was enough time for the little blighters to survive, before removing them to the orphanage. The weaning room was said to be just twenty-eight feet by twelve and held seventy women and children in cramped conditions with sometimes no more than bread and water for sustenance. Diarrhoea and vomiting, caused by the confined and unwholesome room without both fresh air or exercise, was usually the most frequent cause of death among both mother and child, and their deaths were rarely even registered by the Medical Attendant nor was an inquest ever requested. Children were known to spend a minimum of five years in the orphanage, never seeing their mothers again although they were possibly just on the other side of the wall, before being sent back to the mainland to go into service, or in rare cases to be adopted. Hilda was told of women finishing their sentence and going back to England without so much as looking for the poor bastards that they had brought into this wretched world.

They were led through the hospital ward that housed the broken women and children, who coughed violently and lay near death with their transparent skin draped ghostly over their frail bones. Hilda had to cover her nose from the smell of defecation and vomit that soiled the beds. She wasn't the only one. There were two exhausted looking nurses standing at the end of the row of beds, handkerchiefs covering their noses and mouths, their eyes bloodshot and hands covered in sores from the constant contact with the ill, and little to no cleaning solutions to keep them safe.

"These are your fill-ins," The Task Mistress said kindly to the nurses. "They aren't the strongest looking lot we asked for, but it's something." She touched one of the nurses on the arm and motioned for the twenty women to keep following her. At the end of a long hall, they were ushered into a small room with bunk style beds and sheets hanging across ropes as dividers. Hospital style dresses were neatly folded on the ends of half the beds and cooking dresses with aprons and bonnets on the other half. Hilda immediately took a bed with the cook uniforms, believing that to be a much safer place than the hospital.

A large, angry looking woman pushed a trolley into the room and started dishing stew into small bowls.

"You will eat now," said the Task Mistress looking at them all, "and at first light you will get to work. You will do twelve hours each day while the days are longer, to prepare us for the winter. Eat now then sleep." She walked out of the room leaving a constable standing at the door on guard, until the women all held a bowl of food. Hilda watched the cook push her trolley out of the door and converse briefly with the constable. He took something out of his pocket that looked like a small bag of grain and handed to the cook. She stuffed it in her apron pocket and waddled off. He then slammed the door and set the bolt on the other side.

16

Eadlin sat in the tea rooms trying to concentrate on Lidia and Rose's in-depth story about a new dress store in town but found, ever since the day at the Port, she struggled to concentrate on even the simplest of tasks or conversations. She had tried to go back to her normal daily routine but felt it quite pointless and without meaning now. She nodded her head at the moments she thought it was expected and consoled at the moments it seemed needed, but she didn't have a clue what they were talking about. Over her friend's shoulder and out on the street she saw a man leaning against a wall and looking right at her. It took her a few moments to realise it was the old man from the Port, and she stood suddenly and upended her cup of tea onto the crisp white tablecloth.

"Eadlin?" her friend questioned, "Are you quite alright? You look as if you have seen a ghost." Eadlin's friend was mopping up the tea and waving for assistance. The other ladies in the room were whispering behind their delicate gloved hands to one another.

Eadlin saw the man walk off slowly, and she threw her napkin down and proceeded to push her way past the waiter to get out of the door. She saw the man making his way down the street, not hurrying at all, and occasionally looking behind himself to see if she was following. It was considered unseemly to rush if you were a lady, but that had gone out the window with Eadlin now and she gathered her dress up to a level that exposed her ankles and set out at almost an awkward jog. Dangerously racing across the road in front of the horses and carts, she twisted her ankle when her foot went into a pothole. She stopped mid traffic and looked at her foot in the muddy water and the heel broken off her shoe and cursed to herself. Reaching down she took her shoe off and hobbled across the road, her perfectly white silk stockings now the colour of horse dung. The man rounded the corner, and she rushed to follow. Eadlin found him standing in the side alley next to the Red Lion Inn. She looked at him confused.

"I'm sorry missus, I didn't mean to make you run but I know you are with that Mr Drew, I seen ya the other day at the port, like." He was standing there looking sheepish and wringing his cap in his hands. "My thinking is he'd be the one holding the money, big fella like that."

"Mr Brown," Eadlin said quietly after getting her breath back, "I beseech you to help me. This is my mother we are talking about, whom I miss dearly. And Mr Drew is my oldest dearest friend in the world and, although he has not spoken of it to a soul, he is deeply in love with my mother, so if you know anything of her true whereabouts I beg you to tell us both, and if it is the truth I will pay you as much as I can possibly afford."

The inn's side door to the alley swung open with force, and Angus raced straight for the stranger, and picked him up by the neck fearing he meant to do Eadlin harm. He was just about to punch the man when Eadlin grabbed his elbow and begged him to stop. Angus lowered the cowering form but held his shirtfront just in case.

"Angus this is the man from the Port," she said, slowly noting Angus looking her up and down, as she stood there in an alley with one shoe in her hand talking to a stranger. Momentarily his brain caught up and he looked to the man with stern eyes.

"You'll not be getting away this time you bit faker..." Angus was ready to throttle the man, but Brown put up his hands in surrender.

"Settle down now big fella," he looked up at Angus and pleaded. "I'll tell you all I know, if you fill my poor belly with some of your good rum."

Angus looked to Eadlin, and she nodded. "Well, we're not going in here," Angus motioned to the Red Lion Inn over his shoulder, "what'll the patrons say of Eadlin being seen with the likes of you."

Eadlin looked to the ground, embarrassed by Angus's words.

"I hear tell she's been seen in there with the likes of you son," Mr Brown replied indignantly.

"That's enough, the pair of you. I simply can't go in there looking like this," she said looking down at her muddy feet, "no matter which of you I go in with." She had her hands on her hips now and the men were looking to the ground like young boys. "Angus, go back inside and get a few bottles of the rum and the ale. And you Mr Brown will stay exactly where you are and wait for Mr Drew. If you move, you will get nothing. I will make my way home before I am seen and meet you both there." Eadlin nodded and stormed off out of the alley leaving the two men standing there in silence.

Back at the house, Eadlin moved about her bedroom quickly redressing with the help of her housekeeper, Mrs Hill, tottering around her questioning Eadlin's life choices. She had done as she was asked and sent the other servants out for the night, and helped Miss Eadlin get out of her shockingly grubby stockings without too many questions, but now she insisted on knowing why Mr Drew and a strange man were expected at the house.

"You won't believe me if I tell you, dear Gabby," as she fondly referred to her housekeeper and past nanny.

"Why don't you try me then child, I may surprise you." Mrs Hill smiled at Eadlin in a calm motherly fashion.

"Mr Drew and I never believed father's story of mother being mugged and killed." She looked at the shocked look on Mrs Hill's face. "Never, not even from the start, and now a man has come to us with proof. He tells us, that mother is still alive." Eadlin spoke fast at the end, lest Mrs Hill try to stop her.

"My child!" Mrs Hill had her hand across her mouth and her eyes wide. She paused for several breaths before speaking again. "Can this man be trusted?"

"What do you mean, can this man be trusted?" Eadlin stopped in her movements. "I have just told you something quite extraordinary, that I thought you might at least argue with me about, and that is the only question you ask me?"

"Well dear, we do tend to discuss things amongst the help between the houses, and there was a growing concern that something seemed a little...off." Mrs Hill looked sheepish.

"And you did not think to mention it to me. What has been said?... Oh, don't worry about it now, they will be here soon. But we will discuss this at length in the morning." Eadlin kept getting dressed with Mrs Hill's help until the servant's doorbell at the rear of the house chimed. They both hustled down the spiral staircase that went to the kitchen and burst open the door, to Angus and Mr Brown's surprise. Eadlin dragged them both in and Mrs Hill poked her head out the door making sure nobody was watching. Eadlin put four cups on the table and snatched the bottles out of Angus's hands. Mrs Hill pushed Mr Brown into his seat and started pouring the drinks.

"I am sorry to rush you both, but we only have a while to talk before the staff come back," Eadlin explained herself to their confused expressions. She sat primly and waited for Mr Brown to drink his fill, his eyes watching her warily over his upturned cup. Eventually, he slowly put it on the table and cleared his throat.

"It was six or so months back now when my two cousins and I were asked to jump a lady, change her into slops and drop her off at the women's holdings down on the port." He swallowed nervously looking at the anger on Angus's face.

"Keep talking," Angus said with a low growl.

"And well, my cousin told me the job was called off, like, and I thought nothin more of it till I see's him flashing about some new slops and the like." Mr Brown emptied his rum and Eadlin filled it up immediately to keep him going. "And I was like, what's all this then, Charlie, 'cause that's his name, Charlie."

Mrs Hill was rolling her eyes and Mr Brown took offence. "Here lady, I said I was going to tell the truth so don't get all uppity with me."

"Enough you two," Eadlin said looking to them both and patting Mr Brown's hand. "Do go on." She smiled sweetly and kicked Mrs Hill under the table gently.

"Well, the three of us get into a quarrel don't we, 'cause I worked out they was cutting me out of my share to have more for themselves. So, I comes round here and decided I would do the right thing, yeah? And let you know you been had and the like."

Angus stood quickly and grabbed Mr Brown by the scruff of his neck and reared back his arm and fist, spilling the cups on the table. Eadlin stood at the same time and grabbed Angus by the elbow, not for the first time today, and he let go and paced around the kitchen. Mr Brown was looking from Eadlin to Angus with startled eyes.

"Mr Brown," she cooed to smooth the tension, "Do go on."

"Well, I will if you control that beast," he said pointing at Angus. "I am just trying to do the Christian thing here."

Eadlin stood the cups up and poured herself a large splash of rum. Sculling it in one sip, she controlled her regorge and felt the burn down her chest. She took several deep breaths and filled all the cups, handing Mr Brown his and motioning for him to carry on.

"So, I took the hat off Charlie and brought it to you as proof. Mrs Perry isn't dead. Charlie watched her get put on the Charlotte, a privately owned goods hulk that carries convicts for the government as a side hustle."

"Convicts!" Eadlin was astounded. "How could they ever think my mother was a convict?" Now Eadlin was pacing the kitchen and Angus had sat down.

"Why would the Judge believe Hilda was a convict?" He snapped at Mr Brown.

"That I do not have the answer to, my good man." Mr Brown was starting to get a little drunk. "Now, do you have my money?"

"I thought you were telling Miss Eadlin this to be a good Christian?" Mrs Hill asked sarcastically.

"Even good Christians, such as I, need to live, deary." He smiled at her sweetly and she left the table shaking her head. Angus counted out several notes and shoved them into Mr Brown's inside jacket pocket and, lifting him up by the lapel, walked him to the door. Angus shoved him outside and he fell on his backside and smiled up at Angus. "Pleasure doing business with you, good sir," he slurred, and wobbled off into the dark night.

Angus walked back to the table and saw Eadlin sitting with her face in her hands crying.

"Are you alright, lass?" he asked and bent down on one knee in front of her.

She lifted her head, and he could see she was laughing, and crying at the same time. Way too many emotions for Angus to work out.

"Absolutely perfect Angus, absolutely perfect."

17

Hilda moved about the industrial sized kitchen mechanically doing her set chores of peeling potatoes and carrots. She was thinking about June and her instant posting with the soldier, and how sad it had been to watch her walk away from the Sydney yard. June had looked over her shoulder at Hilda until the couple had turned a corner, tears in her eyes also. Hilda missed June dearly but prayed her life was going well.

Living here at the factory had become tedious for Hilda although she knew she was better off than the other ladies, hearing their stories late at night of the sick and the dying, the cramped conditions and the orphanage that had no love for the unwanted children. Many of the women cried woefully at night, making it hard to get to sleep.

Hilda felt, rather than saw, Mrs Webb standing before her with her hands on her rounded hips.

"Are we off in a fairy land again, Hilda?" she mocked. "You've been holding that one potato so long its growing sprouts." She turned away, laughing at her joke.

"I was just thinking of a dear friend, Mrs Webb; she got assigned straight away to an ex-soldier. I hope she is all right," Hilda replied and carried on with her peeling.

Mrs Webb, as it turned out, had not just been the large woman who had bought the women their first meal when they had arrived at this hell hole, but was also in charge of the kitchen, seeing out her last of seven years. She had explained to her new appointees, the way *she* liked to run things and that if anyone jeopardised her remaining time here, they would find themselves on the menu for the pigs. Not willing to test her on that made the kitchen the quietest and safest place to work.

"I should think she's having the time of her life," Mrs Webb replied sarcastically and kept stirring the enormous cast iron pot sitting on the fire.

"I met the soldier when we were on the ship. He seemed quite fond of her, and she is a very strong and clever woman." Hilda felt defensive.

"If she was clever, she wouldn't have got caught." Mrs Webb swiped half a tonne of diced onion off a cutting board into the pot and wiped her brow with her arm. "And I've yet to meet a soldier of good character out here," she said, waving the wooden spoon at Hilda as she spoke.

"I wasn't suggesting he was of good character, just that she would be more than able to deal with him," Hilda was standing up now getting annoyed. "And you are here, so you must have got caught too?"

"I was framed, actually." She went reflectively quiet for a moment and stared into the pot. "I had a good business once. In a quiet little town. We had a boarding house and tearoom." She looked up at Hilda. "We, meaning my husband and I." She shook her head.

"What happened?" Hilda asked quietly.

"A bit-faker came to town and convinced my husband that we had the perfect spot to be selling a little rum on the side." She walked off out of the kitchen and into the small garden that housed the herbs. Hilda waited till she returned.

"My husband was a lazy man and easy to convince that he would make more money with less effort if he sold the rum." She shredded the parsley into the pot. "And to make a long story short, when the bobbies came around, he left out the back door, leaving me to take the punishment."

"I am sorry to hear your story, I really am." Hilda sat and kept peeling the potatoes. The kitchen was silent for a few moments, and all that could be heard was the plopping bubbles in the giant pot.

"I know your story too, Hilda. There are no secrets here." She was looking at Hilda again with pity in her eyes. "I can understand how you feel, betrayal by someone you loved and trusted is the hardest of all betrayals."

Hilda looked at Mrs Webb and said nothing.

Mrs Webb sighed deeply and continued, "I will sail back to England at the end of my sentence and seek my revenge. I will not let what my husband did to me go unpunished, and neither should you. Use it Hilda, use that anger that I can see coursing through your blood to get you through this terrible time."

Mrs Webb used the shovel to drag the burning logs out from below the pot and put them in the steel bucket. She called to another woman to help her lift the bucket with a long stick and they took the smoking hot ashes out into the garden, leaving Hilda to think on that advice. She had never been a malicious person, never really had to. She had gone fifty years thinking the person she was would be enough for her husband, and the course she was on would stay straight. And now she was sitting here feeling like somehow her moorings to life had been undone, and she was drifting away from her old self. She had taken pride in everything she had done, and in the end it still wasn't enough for some people. She'd finished crying now, silently in her sleep and in moments when no one was looking. Her heart still ached but she kept it to herself. Every woman here had a heartache of their own.

She was broken out of her thoughts by Mrs Webb standing before her again.

"Come with me, Hilda." She said and headed out the door again. Hilda followed like a curious child, glad for the distraction. They rounded the vegetable garden all the way to the high concrete wall that was covered with vines. Mrs Webb stood with her back to the wall and looked around briefly, so Hilda did the same.

"Do you know what a bolter is, Hilda?" she whispered out the side of her mouth.

"No," Hilda copied.

"It's what they call the runaway convicts. Even if they are caught, they are still called bolters, so the other guards know they must keep an eye on them."

Hilda looked to Mrs Webb suddenly and saw her crawl through the tangle of vines effortlessly and disappear. She stepped sideways to where Mrs Webb had stood and looked around the garden one more time, reaching behind herself to touch the wall, but behind the vines was nothing. Her hand went straight through, and she was grabbed on the other side by Mrs Webb who yanked her roughly through. She fell on her stomach on the other side and looked up at the grey wall in confusion.

"Keep very quiet Hilda, and stand up," Mrs Webb whispered and watched Hilda slowly stand and look at her. "I found this hole by accident just the other day whilst searching for the berries in the vine."

"Are we outside the factory?" Hilda whispered in excitement and watched Mrs Webb nod.

"Oh, Hilda, if I had found this hole years ago, I would not be here now, but I am so close to leaving, I dare not." Mrs Webb grabbed Hilda's hands, "But you, you can go and find your way back home. Get your revenge while the fire still burns in you."

"But how will I get back? I barely know how I even got here?" Hilda was excited and afraid at the same time.

"I can pack you what you need, food blankets and boots. You must head to the port and find a way back to the mainland. Do whatever it takes to get on a ship and save yourself." Mrs Webb stuck her head back through the hole and then looked back at Hilda. "Come now, this isn't the time, we need to be ready. Winter is coming and it's a bitter cold that blows through here. You must be prepared."

"But what of the soldiers, surely I will be caught straight away?" Hilda was getting nervous.

"The soldiers are lazy in winter and will leave it a few days to see if you freeze to death." She crawled back through the hole and motioned for Hilda to follow from the other side. After they were through, they stood for a moment and cleaned off their clothes of sticks and leaves. Hilda turned to see Mrs Webb staring at her intently.

"If anyone has the stomach to make a run for it, lass, it is you." Mrs Webb wandered off back to the kitchen at a slow, thoughtful pace, arms behind her back, watching the ground as she walked.

18

Angus looked out at the vast ocean and wondered about the monsters from the deep. He'd been told some dark stories in his youth, and having never been a sea faring man, he'd never thought of them since. All the sailors on board were fanatically superstitious, so he had to assume the stories he had heard must be true. He shivered slightly and felt for the dagger he had sheathed in his belt rings.

He thought of the argument he had had with Eadlin on leaving, when she had demanded to come with him to Australia. Eadlin had her mother's tenacious, pig-headed temperament, and when he had put his foot down and refused to let her come the conversation had gotten heated, to put it mildly. He had pleaded with her to understand that it was not a safe journey nor a destination for a young lady, and he wasn't sure he could protect her around such evil willed men. She had relented in the end and bought the one passenger ticket for Angus, and proceeded to sulk as he waved her goodbye.

He wasn't expected to do anything on the hulk under the passenger ticket, but it had been a couple of months into the trip, and he was bored rigid. He had busied himself at the start with talking to the sailors and the captain about the convicts; where they were sent and how they were treated, without raising too much suspicion. The captain had told him the hulk that brought the last lot of women over had been the Charlotte, and that the captain, who was known to be a cruel, sadistic man, had been court marshalled for the mismanagement of the convicts in his care. Apparently nothing came of the court martial because the judge was the captain's cousin.

Angus had been told a great number of the female convicts had died on that trip and it left him sleepless to be told no one knew any names. He wrote down everything he was told so he could send it back in a letter to Eadlin once they docked at Rio De Janeiro, as was his promise to her to get her to stay. But he left out the story of the women dying; it was too soon into his journey to think the worst and no point therefore worrying Eadlin unnecessarily.

Angus woke one morning from being rolled around on his bunk. He noticed his bedding was on the floor and the other passengers' hammocks were rocking back and forth. The temperature seemed to have dropped overnight, leaving a damp chill in the air. He rose quickly and dressed as best as he could with the movement of the boat and opened the heavy door to the deck, letting go as the wind ripped it out of his fingers and slammed it against the outer wall. He saw the sailors on deck all hurrying about with furrowed brows and intensity in their work, so he went up to one he was familiar with and questioned what was going on.

"We're nearing the dreaded Cape of Good Hope, sir," yelled the sailor over the ever-increasing roar of the ocean. "Captain says we're sailing into a storm the likes of nothing he's seen before." The sailor's eyes were popping with anxiety as he looked at Angus, then quickly pointed towards the small speck of land they could see to the left. "That over there is the Union of South Africa," then he pointed out to sea further, "And that be the cape waters that belong to the Flying Dutchman."

Angus looked around and saw that everyone was listening now. Their faces white. He now understood the level of superstition that ran their lives.

"The Flying Dutchman?" he cleared his throat and asked with interest.

"Tis' said the captain, van der Decken, in 1641 wasn't concentrating on the storm coming in 'cause he wanted to start a colony over on the land, see? So, he's in the quarter galleries, writing letters and such, but in the distance the storm was blowing the waves up to a height of thirty feet or more, and the captain wasn't ready. The storm came in fast and pushed the boat against the rocks and they all perished, and now she lies at the pit of this merciless ocean. It's said on a foggy day you can see the ship, floating just above the water, see, that be where she gets the name from, and hearing the captain yelling out he'll make it to land one day." The sailor shivered at the end of his tale.

"Are we coming into such a storm?" Angus asked.

"Aye, that we are." The sailor pointed around himself and said to Angus with kindness, "There's much to be done to get her ready. A big lad like yourself could be very handy right now?"

"Of course," Angus replied immediately, "Tell me what to do."

The sailor handed Angus some ropes and told him where to tie them off. The wind had picked up even more and there was a slight menacing roar to it, like a challenge, Angus thought. The rain had gotten heavier, and the drops were getting bigger making his sodden shirt stick to his body. Waves were starting to crash over the quarter deck making it hard to move about. Loose objects were starting to slide back and forth with the rolling of the ship, and Angus could see the other passengers peering out at him from behind the safety of the cabin door. It wasn't just the women and the children, there were able bodied men in there too, and Angus shook his head at their weakness.

He felt a sailor's hand on his shoulder as he held onto the mainmast for dear life. "Take yourself inside now, lad," the sailor yelled, and spat sea water.

"No!" Angus roared, "I can still be of some assistance. I'm not afraid."

They both looked to the sterncastle deck and watched the captain yelling into the wind. "Strike the royals!" he bellowed, and the sailors moved to the masts. "Batten the hatches and reef the mainsail!"

Angus looked up just in time to see the wind rip off the Admiral's pennant from the top of the mainsail mast, then there was a loud crack as the mizzen topgallant sail ripped free. The captain had taken a zig zag course now, going from a larboard tack to a starboard tack, to keep the boat from heading towards land and an imminent demise. Angus held on with one hand and wiped the salty waves from his burning eyes. The ship rose and fell, rolled and bashed through the waves, taking sailors overboard that hadn't harnessed themselves to something sturdy. The passenger's door was struck with flying debris and burst open, ripping off its hinges and flying over the side. Inside Angus could see terrified faces staring at him in horror, before he was hit with something to the back of his head. His body slumped to the deck and flailed about with the boat, and the ropes around his midsection cut into his skin.

19

Hilda shivered in the ice-cold morning air, slowly losing the feeling in her fingers and toes. She had made it through the damp forest beyond the garden wall, only hurting herself a few times as she tripped over fallen logs and slid down deep embankments. Her heart had been racing, and it had kept her warm through the night, to keep her pushing on and not stop. She had heard the alarm sound of her escape in the distance, but it had been muffled by the mountains, so she hadn't let it worry her.

Squatting down now behind the building on the port, she could see the vessel she needed to be on to get back to Sydney Cove. Mrs Webb had told her if she could get that far undetected, there was a sailor she knew that could get her on a returning hulk back to England.

People meandered on and off the boat, loading it with supplies for the mainland. It was not a passenger ship so she would have to stow away somewhere in the goods hull and pray not to be found.

She saw her chance when several rum barrels and wooden boxes were put near the loading ramp. Dressed in men's clothes, with her hair all tucked under her flat cap, she felt hopeful she would pass as a dock worker. She dashed quietly towards the barrels and hid while she surveyed her surroundings. Still in the clear, she stood slowly and picked up a box and followed another worker as he tipped one of the barrels on its metal edge and start rolling it up the slight incline of the wood platform. Her arms were starting to shake with the weight of the box, but the worker was too busy keeping the barrel rolling to notice her sudden appearance. Her panic was starting to set in at the thought of being caught and she had to calm herself mentally.

One of the workers came out of the hull and mumbled a morning greeting to her, making her freeze on the spot, but he barely looked up at her and walk off down the platform. Hilda picked up her pace even faster down into the hull, dropped the box casually and, finding a pile of wool filled sacks against the edge, dove behind them. She was sure her pounding heart could be heard and would give her away as she sat and tried to get comfortable. She hadn't eaten for two days now, and her stomach ached as it rumbled. She sat in her hiding place and waited the long hours it took to load the vessel. Every chance she got she built an igloo type cave with the wool bags so that she was hidden from sight completely. Voices rose and fell as they came and went, and lastly she heard horse hooves on the wooden floorboards. Surely they load the livestock last, she thought to herself, eager to set sail. The main thing was she was warm and dry and moderately comfortable.

At some point unbeknown to Hilda, she fell asleep. The warmth, quiet and rocking of the ship must have done it. She dreamt of home and her daughter. Of Angus and the Inn.

She woke sleepily and tried to stretch out. When her legs touched the wool bales she was reminded of her surroundings and sat up wide awake. She heard the water under the boat, mice rustling around and the horses snorting. There was also a quiet conversation coming closer to her hiding spot. Something about one of the voices was familiar to her and she strained herself to hear it better. Then her blood froze.

"The horses will be collected by the governor's man when we arrive," Captain Drake spoke, patting one horse on the rump. "Give them a brush down now and have them ready, a gift for his wife or some such thing." He sounded bored and walked closer to Hilda's fort. She held her breath for what seemed an impossible time, listening to him touch the wool bale.

"Keep one of these aside for me, John, there's a good fellow." Slowly Hilda heard them both leave and close the barn style door, and she let out her breath too loudly, making the horses scuff their hooves for a moment. They were trotting back and forward in their enclosure making whinnying noises, so Hilda rose to calm them. Her sudden movement made them more skittish, bringing the sailor into the hull. He saw her immediately and stopped in his tracks.

"What have we got here then?" he asked out loud "We've got ourselves a stow away." He strode purposely towards Hilda with a wicked look on his face, making her bound out of her hiding spot and run to the other side of the room. "Come on lad," he laughed "Captain has a special way he treats stow aways." He chased her around the room until she was cornered, grabbing her by her jacket and throwing her onto her back side. She landed hard with her elbows connecting painfully on the timber floor, and her flat beret falling off her head. The sailor stopped short at the sight of her long blonde hair and let out a slow whistle.

"Well look at what we have here then?" he smirked and laughed to himself. "Normally I would keep you down here as my personal little plaything, but Captain Drake is not one to mess about with. Pity though." He sighed to himself and grabbed Hilda by her hair and yanked her painfully into standing position. He smirked slowly and ran his tongue up her cheek. The reek of his breath made her turn her head away in disgust, while her hands tried to release his fist from her hair. His lust overcame him, and he pushed Hilda forward over the boxes, and separating her feet with a kick he began to roughly pull at the breeches she was wearing.

"That will be enough, John, release the wench." Captain Drake stood behind them, calm yet menacing. The sailor turned, still holding Hilda's hair in his fist, looking guilty. He was about to explain himself when the captain raised a hand to silence him and stared at Hilda, first in disbelief, then in humour.

His face went serious again. "Get me the chains," he said to John, who ran off nodding. When they were alone, the captain walked closer to Hilda, causing her to step backwards until there was nowhere to go. His expression was blank as he stood so close to her, her face was nearly touching his chest. She felt his breath on the top of her head as she kept her eyes to the ground.

"It's been a long time, Mary Cooper," he breathed. "Too long." He was silent for a while and Hilda whispered.

"My name is not Mary Cooper."

"What?" he said a little louder, making Hilda throw her head back and look him in the eyes.

Through gritted teeth she snarled, "My name is not bloody Mary Cooper. My name is Hilda Perry. I have committed no crime to be in this hell hole and nothing, and I mean nothing, will stop me from escaping and reaping my revenge for this injustice." Her nostrils were flaring, and her chest rose and fell.

A slow smile spread across his face. Amused and aroused by her fiery outburst, he couldn't help but run his hand up her stomach and onto her breast. She pushed him back and slapped his face, forcing him to grab her wrists and pull her close again. He bent down to whisper in her ear, "Bolter, you're mine now."

20

Angus woke up with a start, the memory of the storm still vivid in his mind. The ship he had been on was nowhere to be seen. He found himself washed ashore on a deserted beach, surrounded by debris from the wreck. The sky was clear now, a stark contrast to the raging tempest that had nearly claimed his life.

With a groan, he pulled himself to his feet, scanning the horizon. He had to find another ship, and quickly. Australia was still miles away, and he had no intention of being stranded here. He began to walk along the shore; his eyes peeled for any signs of habitation or vessels.

After what felt like hours, he spotted smoke in the distance. Hope flared in his chest as he quickened his pace, heading towards what he hoped was a bustling port town. As he drew nearer, the outlines of ships docked along the wharf came into view. The town was bustling with activity, sailors and merchants going about their business.

Angus approached a grizzled old sailor who was overseeing the loading of crates onto a ship.

"Excuse me," Angus called out. "I need passage to Australia. Can you help me?"

The old sailor looked him up and down, his weathered face unreadable. "Australia, eh? That's a long way off, lad. But you're in luck. The 'Southern Star' is setting sail for Sydney at dawn. You'll have to speak to Captain Harrington."

"Thank you," Angus said, relief washing over him. He made his way to the 'Southern Star', a sturdy-looking vessel anchored at the end of the dock. Captain Harrington, a tall man with a commanding presence, was giving orders to his crew.

"Captain Harrington!" Angus called out, making his way up the gangplank. "I need to get to Australia. I can work for my passage."

The captain turned to face him, a sceptical look in his eyes. "And why should I take you on, stranger?"

Angus squared his shoulders preparing for a lie. "Because I have skills. I am a carpenter by trade, and I can mend sails and rigging. I will earn my keep."

The captain considered him for a moment, then nodded. "Alright, you have got yourself a deal. Be on board by dawn, and do not be late. We have a long voyage ahead of us."

Angus nodded gratefully, shaking the captain's hand. He had a new hope now, a new chance to continue his journey. As he walked away to find food and rest, he could not help but think of Hilda, wondering where she was and if their paths would cross again.

* * *

Thankfully, Angus was a fast learner and the journey went quickly. The captain kept him busy maintaining the sails or doing maintenance below deck. The hard work made his body feel stronger as the time wore on and in no time at all he had found his sea legs. There were fierce storms along the way that left the ship needing ongoing repairs and calm afternoons which allowed the sailors to sit and drink rum and reminisce on past journeys. Angus was sure towards the end he would have become a sailor if his life had have been different.

Late one evening, Angus sat in the moonlight and enjoyed the sleeping hush that covered the boat. Finally, a moment to think. He realised in his rush to be here, he had not even thought out a plan of attack for when he landed in Sydney Cove. What little money he had been given by Eadlin had washed out to sea and he was left with nothing to barter with. His only trade was that of a brewer, and perhaps on the colonies that was not such a bad thing to know.

He massaged the back of his head out of habit now, where he had been struck during the storm on the last ship, and felt the scab still in his hair. It was no longer tender to the touch, and he was grateful the wound had eventually stopped seeping. The captain had told him earlier that they still had eighteen days more of sailing, which wasn't so bad after what he'd been through so far. He settled back into his hammock and let the slow waves rock him to sleep, drenched in the glow of the full moon.

21

Hilda had spent the trip across the Tasman Sea chained up in a small hold. She had a mattress of hay and meals supplied regularly but had not seen the lecherous captain since he had whispered to her in the hull. Her mind went back to his behaviour aboard the convict ship and now she had to agree with her friend June, what the devil was he playing at? Instead of being satisfied to be left alone, she was left on edge every time someone simply passed her door. It was frustrating, and she thought he may be doing it on purpose, like a game of some sorts.

They arrived at Sydney Cove to loud horns, which she assumed was some sort of signal of an incoming ship, and the boat slowed to a near standstill. She had no window to look out of, so had to listen intently to noises outside and try and decide when her door would be opened. The boat would have to dock at the newly built jetty to unload the animals, so she listened out for that. Sure enough, after some heavy banging and men yelling, her door was yanked open and there stood Captain Drake. He reached into her hold and dragged her out by the chains that bound her wrists. He was behaving unnecessarily rough with her, making her wonder if it was all for show.

Two soldiers walked up the low ramp, all pompous in their red uniforms, and handed the captain a letter, at which he pushed Hilda into their hands, and they dragged her off the ship. She turned at the bottom and looked back at the captain, surprised to see a satisfied smirk on his face, confusing her even more. She tried to ask the soldiers what was to become of her now, but they just ignored her and dragged her along, through the town, and back to the nursing station she had been in once before.

"Ah! It is the mysterious Mary Cooper again," the matron said with a kind smile. "Hand her over then," she snapped at the soldiers, "I haven't got all day."

She took Hilda into the cool hospital and snapped her finger for her first nurse. "Get her cleaned up again and bring her to my office. Off you go girl, don't give us any trouble now."

Hilda watched the matron leave and turned to follow the nurse. A warm bath was laid with the heavenly scent of eucalypt filling the air. "What will they do to me?" she asked the nurse, as she lowered her sore body into the water. She winced at the pain when the water touched the cuts on her hands and wrists and the skinning on her elbows.

"You'll be considered a bolter now, Miss," the nurse whispered and looked to the door quickly. "I've heard tell they treat bolters real bad, well the men anyways. I've never heard of a lady bolter, none of us have." She looked back to Hilda and squatted lower to her face. "Everybody is talking about you Miss, what to do with a woman bolter, you're famous." The nurse stood quickly and moved about the room getting towels ready. She helped Hilda dress in clean clothes and tended to her cuts with bandages and salve. "Follow me, please," she whispered and smiled.

Hilda was led into the matron's personal office. It was whitewash walls and large windows that let the light in, making it a cheery room with plants in baskets and the smell of fresh tea.

"Take a seat, Mary Cooper. Or are you really Mary Cooper?" the matron handed Hilda a cup of tea and biscuits and sat opposite her, her eyebrow raised in query.

"I have been trying to tell everyone that is not my name, but no one will listen," Hilda said feeling exhausted.

"I have been in nursing since I was a very young girl, and I have learnt that teeth and skin such as yours, do not exist in the same world as these other women. Oh no, that is for sure."

"I was framed, back in England, by my husband's mistress," Hilda stood and paced the room, finally able to tell her story. "I was mugged, drugged, stripped of my clothes and left at the women's watchtower. The judge wouldn't listen to me, and I was whipped for making a scene." Hilda turned to the matron, "Can you help me?"

The matron shook her head sadly. "Most of the women who come here have been done wrong by their men folk. I have heard such terrible stories in my time. I could tell you I will try to help you, but I have been here long enough to know that what I have to say bears no weight around here. I'm sorry."

Hilda slumped back into the chair, defeated.

"The best I can do is keep an eye on you. Help you stay safe." Matron was rubbing her brow now and Hilda had a feeling she knew her fate.

"What is it?" she urged "What will they do to me?"

"You are to go before the judge tomorrow, lass. I will come too and hopefully be of some strength for you. It is the most I can do." The matron looked at Hilda and waited for her to weep but she was surprised to see the fire in Hildas' eyes, the defiant look of a women who refused to be broken.

22

"Mary Cooper, you have been charged with the colonial offence of absconding from the women's factory in Van Dieman's Land, stowing away on a government ship, immoral conduct and insolence." The magistrate barked. "The punishment for such abhorrent behaviour is to put you in the service of government or any inhabitant of the colonies. Your head will be shaved, and you will be sent to solitary confinement for a term not exceeding fourteen days, then placed in a neck collar for a period not exceeding seven days and then confinement to hard labour, not exceeding three calendar months."

Hilda looked to her left and saw Matron staring back at her with astonishment. She wanted to pass out and throw up at the same time. She wanted to scream and run for her life. But matron stared at her intently, tipped the bottom of her chin up and signalled at Hilda to stay strong. So, she took several breaths, turned back to the bench, and kept her expression courtly.

She watched the man next to the magistrate whisper something to him and then point to someone behind Hilda in the courtroom.

"Ah! Captain Drake. I am told you have applied to take the convict to your settlement and carry out the courts wishes?" The magistrate looked over the papers handed to him. "Everything seems to be in order."

Hilda looked at the matron in fear. So, this was his game. Unfortunately, the matron herself was in shock for Hilda and failed to be a positive influence this time, the matron looked back at Hilda with the same expression.

Hilda was wrenched to her feet by two soldiers, her wrists clamped back in irons and pulled towards the door of the court. She couldn't see Captain Drake anywhere, as she was shoved into a buggy and taken back to the hospital with the matron.

Neither of them spoke while the matron put together a simple bag of clothes and toiletries for her. A blanket and a shawl. The soldiers looked on as the matron shaved Hilda's head, both of them silently crying now. She lovingly put a bonnet on Hilda's head and tied it under her chin, resting her hands on Hilda's shoulders. "I will keep an eye on you lass, I promise."

Hilda was taken to a buggy enclosed by iron bars and roughly pushed in. She was looking at the matron when Captain Drake rode his horse between them. He smirked at her, while trying to calm his horse which fidgeted about. "Are you ready?" he said to her with malice, as he laughed and rode off ahead of the buggy.

They travelled for several hours through the forest, which Hilda thought would have been most enjoyable were it not for the fact that she was behind metal bars. She spoke to herself sternly, strengthening her resolve, hardening her heart. Let him do what he likes, she thought, I will get away. It will be all I think about.

Up ahead in a clearing she saw a large homestead with smoke coming from three chimneys. A pretty garden with a neat green lawn surrounded the building, and then paddocks with cows in them. Not at all what she was expecting.

A well-dressed woman came out of the house with a convict woman in tow, and she waved to the captain with a posh familiarity. He dismounted his horse and strode up to her and gave her a perfunctory peck on her ivory cheek as he led her back into the house. She was trying to look over her shoulder at Hilda, but he kept her distracted and moved her forward.

Returning moments later, he opened the back of the cage and dragged Hilda out so roughly she stumbled to the dirt.

"Get up mollisher and walk," he spat at her.

Hilda stood and ripped her arm out of his grasp. "You lied to the magistrate before the court case, didn't you? Just so you could keep me your prisoner. You vile man. Do not think for one moment I will become your whore, you pig!"

He grabbed at her again, ignoring her insults, and pushed her towards the horse shed. Inside he took her to a small room that resembled a cell, boarded up with a small window of bars at the front and a trap door. He pushed her inside and chained her to a link on the wall, quickly pinned an iron collar about her neck and stood back to look at his handy work.

"I'll break your English spirit, woman. I'll break you like a dog." He laughed and backed out of the cell, closing the door till it was black as night inside.

Hilda shivered, not at the cold, but at the effort it was taking her to be so strong. The fool had given himself away. His sick little game was to break her. Had he done this sort of thing before? She tried to form a plan in her head, but the iron collar was biting at her skin and weighing down on her collar bones and it had only been on for a few minutes. Tears leaked down her face and she put her head in her hands.

"There's no point crying about it." A soft voice said from the dark.

"Who's there?" Hilda tried to stand quickly making the wrist irons grab at the point in the wall. She fell with groan, shuffling around till her back was against the wall.

"My name is Rosie," she sighed "at least that's what I used to be called. No one calls me anything anymore."

"How old are you girl? Why are you in here?" Hilda was choking up listening to the girl's voice. Her tone was so dismissive and indifferent, calm, as though she no longer cared.

"I don't know how old I am. I came over from the orphanage. I think I'm eight, but I don't really know." She went quiet for a while.

Hilda wiped tears from her eyes. "Why are you here Rosie?" she asked gently.

"I was going to be Mrs Drakes new child, but she said I was too sickly looking and told Mr Drake to get her another one. I even got to spend one night in the bedroom that would have been mine. It was all pink and white and smelled like fresh flowers. But she told the cook she didn't want me in the house no more, so I got sent out here." Her voice cracked ever so slightly as if not getting the pretty room was the saddest part of her tragic story."

"Oh Rosie," Hilda held back a sob. "Are you in chains, dear girl?"

"Only one ankle, can I come sit next to you?" she asked shyly.

Hilda held out her hands in the dark and felt for Rosie. "Of course, I'm over here child." She felt a small hand go into hers, it was cold but soft, and she pulled the child near to her body and wrapped her arms around her thin frame. She smelled vile, and her hair felt like a tangle of hay and sticks. "How long have you been in here Rosie?" she asked.

"I don't know, Missus," was all she replied.

Hilda laid her head back against the wall and listened to the child softly breathe. After a time, her body went limp, and she started to gently snore. What a loathsome world this was, Hilda thought to herself and gently laid the child's head in her lap. She would escape this nightmare and take the child with her, and by God she would make them all pay.

23

Angus walked along the busy jetty in Sydney Cove, trying to keep out of everyone's way. He kept his head down and his flat cap low on his eyes. He had no idea the colonies would be so busy. He investigated each store as he walked further along up the main street. The weather was colder than he had been told, although it was still late winter.

He entered the main goods store and wandered around looking at all the merchandise until he was approached by a tall young lad with an apron over his clothes. He explained to the young man that he was new to the continent and would like to find some work and lodgings, mentioning that he was the head brewmaster of fine ale back in Portsmouth. The young man proceeded to tell him of the several Inns and taverns in the area where he could try, when they were interrupted by a man and a woman asking if their order had come in. He looked to the woman and was surprised she was staring at him with her round hazel eyes. She was dressed well, although obviously working class, and had pale ivory skin and a mass of auburn hair tied neatly behind her head.

"I say, sir, did you say you were a brewmaster by trade? From Portsmouth?"

Her husband stopped speaking to the lad and looked over.

"Yes ma'am," Angus said, tipping the front of his hat to her, and she gave her husband a nudge in the arm. Angus looked at her confused but carried on. "I had a good reference from the last place, but alas our boat went down and took all I had."

"My husband and I are looking for a new brewmaster," she said excitedly. "Dear?" she addressed her husband in a tone of authority and nodded towards Angus. "Do speak with this gentleman."

Angus put his hand out to shake and introduced himself properly. The man's name was Mr. William Day, and his somewhat bossy wife was introduced as Mrs June Day. He went on to tell Angus they had built a tavern on their settlement, for travellers on the way from Sydney to the new settlement in Campbelltown.

"We built it not six months ago in Liverpool, and our brewmaster went and died of scurvy." She sounded indignant.

"It wasn't scurvy, dear, it was just the grippe owing to his weak constitution." He looked to Angus and rolled his eyes. "Most the ex-convicts come away with it." He shrugged his shoulder like he didn't care.

"Would you have lodgings as well?" Angus ignored the marital digging and pressed on.

"Well yes, food and board would come out of your earnings of course. Do you know how to cook? Ye might have to do a bit of that too." Mr William Day had found his balls and was letting Angus know he was the head of the business. But he kept looking nervously at his wife standing next to him for approval, so Angus didn't need to ask.

* * *

The buggy ride to the tavern was not altogether comfortable from Angus's position in the rear, and he would jump off from time to time and walk to save his back. Although the excellent luck of landing both a job and lodgings within minutes of landing in Sydney pleased him, the further out of Sydney itself that they travelled the more he thought this wasn't perhaps what he needed to find Hilda. His plan had been to get a job behind a bar and wait till the clients were inebriated before he started questioning them on the whereabouts of the female convicts.

Still, he didn't need to sleep rough in this weather and his money had all gone out to sea, so he saw no other option. He thought on his new host and knew immediately that Mr Day was ex-soldier, he'd been around soldiers enough in his time, but he couldn't pick the lovely Mrs Day. Her accent was controlled with a slight hint of Cockney twang, which he could tell she was trying to mask. Her body, although feminine had a strength to it that was not often present in genteel women. And her attitude, well, he'd seen the same stubborn determinedness in Hilda. Women who would get through anything and come up fighting. He smiled at the thought.

"Penny for your thoughts, Mr. Drew?" Mrs Day chimed, making him come back to the moment. "If I didn't know any better I would say you were thinking of a lady, with that smile on your face. I am looking forward to hearing your story Mr Drew. Get's a little dull sometimes, don't it Mr. Day." She looked at her husband and pursed her lips before looking up the road again. Angus shook his head and smiled. This was going to be interesting.

24

Hilda's time in solitary was finally over when the courts sent out an appointed official to see if captain Drake was doing as the magistrate had ordered with the prisoner. It was unintentionally timed on one occasion that the captain was away at sea, infuriating him on his return to the property.

But for Hilda, life outside of confinement was just as horrendous. His wife, a miserable, vindictive witch of a woman, was both a horror and a blessing for Hilda. She treated Hilda no better than a stray dog when her husband was away, and yet when he was home she never allowed a moment for him to be alone with Hilda.

She could see how this angered him so and his violent moods would be taken out on the other staff, to the point that everyone loathed seeing him ride through the gates. Hilda was aware of the very possibility he would have done away with his wife, were it not for the fact he had married her for money and status alone. Her father was none other than the local bank manager, who was also becoming aware of captain Drakes ill temper, and frequently visited his daughter out of concern.

After several months of this, it had been masterfully arranged, for his daughter's safety, to have Drake captain another vessel of convicts back from England to put a great distance of sea, land and time between the two.

Hilda was made to work long hours of the day, doing whatever task the mistress thought would be the most uncomfortable for her. She was no longer shackled, and the neck iron had been removed, but she was made to live in the horse shed and stay well away from the house. Mrs Drake had worn the lady's maid down with her constant nagging, and now the child, Rosie, was released to work on the property as well.

At night when they lay on their hay mattresses and nibbled on the food that was smuggled out of the kitchen by the cook, they would discuss their getaway. Hilda would have left sooner, but she needed the child to get stronger, or she would die from the effort of the escape. Working outdoors had put colour back in her skin, and Hilda always gave the child more food than she ate herself.

It was the morning of Drake's departure that she was woken roughly and dragged off her mattress by her hair. It took her moments to realise she had been caught unawares by Drake, almost too late to stumble to her feet and react. She started to scream and struggle, to pull her hair out of his fist, waking Rosie who rushed over and threw herself on Drake's back, clawing at his face with her sharp little nails. She was like a wildling, a broken child gone mad, and their struggle made Drake let go of Hilda's hair. Hilda bounded to her feet but was too late to save the child, as Drake reached behind and flung her off by her ankle. She flew and struck the barn wall, sliding down to the dirt and lay, still. Hilda turned to the captain with hate in her eyes and he grabbed her by her scrawny throat, pushing her backwards into the corner, then tripping her so she too fell to the hard ground. The weight of him falling on top of her winded her momentarily.

Hilda tried to scream again, but Drake had his hand roughly across her mouth. The look in his eyes was devilish and he was smiling and drooling, his face just inches away from hers. He used his other hand to force Hilda's wrists through a loop in a horse rope that was hanging from the wall, and pulled it tightly, binding her hands above her head. Sitting back on his haunches he smiled at her and took his hand from her mouth. She instantly started to scream, and he gave her a blow to the head, knocking her unconscious. He used this time to rip open her bodice, exposing her breasts. Excited he lifted her skirts and tore down her underwear.

He slapped at her face to wake her up.

"Wake up, whore. You will be awake for this and remember that I broke you." His anger was brutal, and he spat as he spoke.

Hilda came to and stared at him in horror. She could feel him beneath her skirts fumbling about and she rolled and kicked and screamed.

There was a pistol gunshot and Drake's body flew forward, landing on Hilda. Blood ran from the back of his head onto her bare breasts, and she started sobbing. She looked up to see Mrs Drake standing in her nightgown, hair askew, pistol still raised.

"I didn't do it for you," she said coldly, staring at Hilda with pure hatred. "You are not the first tramp he has brought here, and you would not have been the last. I have seen the graves under the trees, I knew what was happening. But this time, to try to drug *me*. To try to do away with *me* is something I will not allow." She lowered the pistol slowly and looked over her shoulder at the child.

"Get out," she spat suddenly back at Hilda. "Get out of my sight and take that worthless child with you."

"I will not run," Hilda stood slowly and gathered her clothes about herself. "I will not take the punishment for this." She pointed at Drake's lifeless form on the floor. "You did this. You are both evil, sick people." Hilda was starting to shake with the reality creeping into her body.

Mrs Drake sneered, "No one will believe you mollisher. No-one. Now take the maggot and run before I put a bullet in your skull and call it self-defence."

Hilda walked over to Rosie and lifted her lifeless form into her arms. She turned back to Mrs Drake, straightened her shoulders so as not to appear like she was begging. "We will need to take some bedding and warm clothes; will you allow us that?"

Mrs Drake swung the pistol, pointing towards the corner of the barn. "Take your bedding, take that useless half-dead mule over there too, whatever it takes to get you a long way from my property. I will come back in an hour, and you had better be gone, or God help you."

"Thank you," Hilda said quietly to her leaving form. Mrs Drake turned one last time, a wretch of a woman, broken by love. The hatred had gone from her hollow eyes and her soul had left her body. She turned and shuffled away slowly.

25

Hilda had lain Rosie on the mattress, her tiny heart still beating, and slowly changed her torn clothes. She was gathering spare bedding when the groundsman knocked at the barn door. He stuck his head around gingerly and was shocked to see the sight of Hilda and the wee lifeless child.

"Cook has sent me," he spoke quietly and handed Hilda a basket.

Hilda took the offering and held back the tears. One side of her face was swelling, there was straw through her hair, and she suddenly felt a sadness like giving up.

She watched in silence as the groundsman went over to the old mule and put on a bridle and chest plate. The old nag bit at him while he attached the traces and reins, so he gave it a tap on the nose and wiggled his finger at her. He pulled her out of her enclosure and handed Hilda the reins. She stood holding the horse, staring into huge black eyes that stared back tiredly.

Pushing in a small barrow buggy he attached it to the tracers, filled it with soft hay, then stood and looked at Hilda. They stared at each other quietly for a moment, before he lowered his eyes and left the barn.

"You're not going to be too naughty are you girl?" she whispered to the nag after he had left and stroked the horse's cheek. "I haven't got the energy for that to be honest." Hilda smiled at the horse, and she whinnied, nodding her head a few times. She sniffed at Hilda's face and lowered her head and ate some hay.

Gently Hilda placed the child in the buggy and wrapped her tight in their bedding. She made a nest for the basket and found them an old leather tarp, which she secured across the top of the buggy with ropes to keep Rosie dry. At the door to the barn, she turned to take one look back to the house. Cook was watching her through the kitchen windows, dabbing her eyes and waving, and Mrs Drake was standing in the conservatory window, dressed now in her mourning black with her arms crossed across her chest, staring blankly at Hilda before she turned her back on her.

Hilda pulled gently on the reins and led the horse down the long winding driveway, under the tall Ironbarks and wattles, past the cows slowly chewing their cuds while willy-wagtails hopped up and down their backs.

Hilda had no idea where she was meant to go, so she chose a lesser used track, hoping it would take her to someone who could help her with the child.

She walked all day, stopping only to check on Rosie's breathing and to allow the horse to drink at the river. Night was creeping in, and a slow fog was rolling through the trees. She ate a small portion of their rations and tied the horse to a tree, hidden in the forest. Lifting the tarp just enough to crawl in, she curled her body around the child and fell into a deep sleep.

In the morning, she checked Rosie's breathing, which was getting shallow and slightly rattly. "Oh Rosie, dear child, please be strong. We have got this far together. Don't leave me now." Hilda stroked Rosie's hair for a while before crawling out of the buggy, when she came face to face with a young lad sitting on his horse holding two rabbits by their back legs. It was hard to tell who was more surprised.

"Please, can you help us," Hilda begged him. "I have a child in there who needs to see a doctor very urgently. Do you know where we can find a doctor?"

"The doc lives about two hours walk that way," the young man replied, pointing with his rifle over the hill. "I can show you if you like."

Hilda let a sob escape her mouth and leaned forward, trying to breathe. She looked back at him nodding and smiling, while she undid the reins and gave the old horse a gentle tug forward.

He rode slowly next to her, looking at her from time to time. "What are you doing out here, Missus?" he finally asked.

Hilda stopped her horse and looked up at him. "I am an escaped prisoner," she blurted out. "I was wrongly accused of something back in England and I have been through a year of hell. I just want to get off this damn Island and go home." She let the tears fall quietly.

"Oh yeah," he said sounding unsurprised, "we get that a lot round here. Dad says the prisons are bloody useless and couldn't hold a piss up in a brewery." He smiled at her and kept riding.

Hilda felt a laugh rising in her body, a real laugh, so she let it out. It was music to her ears and made her body feel strong, so she picked up her pace and followed.

26

Angus had been working at the Inn for several weeks, without finding out anything useful from the clientele regarding the female prisoners. There were vague discussions about where the women were sent, what they were made to do and how they were treated better than the men. He had noticed during these conversations that Mrs June Day, overhearing, would become uncomfortable and sometimes leave the bar and go back into the kitchen.

Sometimes she would quiz him about why he always brought up the subject with the patrons, and he would pass it off as just making conversation to keep the punters drinking.

It was one particular night, when some soldiers started talking about a woman that had been caught trying to leave Hobart town by stowing away on a cargo ship. At the mention of Captain Drake, Mrs June Day slowly made her way closer to their table and started clearing their empty pots.

"A woman you say," she asked casually, making Angus look up from his spot behind the bar. "Do you happen to know what this woman looked like."

"Oh aye!" piped up the drunkest soldier, looking to impress the pretty Mrs. "She was a looker for her age, a little thin with long blonde hair. Bit stuck up she was." He looked at the other soldiers and they all nodded.

"The magistrate called her a bolter, didn't he?" another spoke. "First female bolter we've had in these parts."

June looked up at Angus and saw him staring at her. "Angus dear, bring these fine soldiers a round on the house." She waved her arms around accommodatingly.

Angus wasn't sure what she was up to, but did as he was asked.

They all cheered at the free drink and June pressed on, her voice slightly higher than usual. "My goodness, how interesting. And what did they do with the poor wretch?" she simmered.

"Captain Drake took her back to his settlement. Oh, but he's a violent man that one," they all nodded together, "I almost feel sorry for the wench." They sat in silence contemplating that before one of them looked at June quizzically.

"Why do you ask?" he said.

"Oh," she stammered before replying, "We don't get to hear a lot of interesting stories out here," she looked to Angus for help, "do we, Mr Drew?"

"Aye, Mrs Day. Nothing as interesting as a soldier's gruelling day, that's for sure." Angus brought over another round and placed it before them with a pat on the back. That seemed to work, so June slid away, and they changed their story and carried on drinking.

Angus followed June into the kitchen and rounded on her. "What was that about, what are you playing at June?"

He stood close to her, and she had to look up to speak to him. "I'm riding for Sydney town," she said as she fastened her shawl and did up her bonnet."

"It is the middle of the darn night! What could be so important?" he whispered.

"Never you mind. I will be gone three days. Tell Mr Day anything you need to. Tell him it is women's business, that always makes him uncomfortable, just do not let him follow me."

Outside she yelled for young Michael, who tended the horses, to get the single buggy ready, and she lit a lantern. Putting her hand on Angus's large chest she looked him in the eyes. "I'll be alright, Angus, please trust me."

Angus was busy cleaning out the mash tubs on the grass when June rode her buggy along the back of the Inn. She looked tired and drawn out, her eyes swollen underneath from grief. He rushed over at the same time as Michael, to help her dismount and walked her into the kitchen.

"Where is Mr Day?" she asked through her weariness.

"Making a delivery. Where have you been June, what is going on?" He poured her a cup of tea and sat waiting while she took a sip.

"Oh Angus," she wailed, "I must tell you something. I was on the last female convict ship to come to Sydney, and I was one of the lucky ones to be taken into service by Mr Day. He was a soldier on the ship, and I convinced him to take me in, so I didn't have to go to the female factories. It feels so selfish of me now; I cannot stand to hear the stories of what the other women have endured." She looked to her hands and sighed before she looked back to him. "My dear friend was on that ship, and I left her at the female's hospital and walked away." June had started sobbing now. "And I never knew what had become of her. I think of her every day."

Angus was not sure where this was going, but his own curiosity was aroused.

"You were on the Charlotte?" he finally asked incredulously.

"Yes, why. Have you heard of it?" she had stopped crying now and looked at him confused.

"Oh June!" he sighed and lowered his head shaking it. "That is the ship I am looking for, that is the ship that took my Hilda away!" He had her arms in his large hands now, trying not to shake her. "I have been trying to find her and here you were the whole time. If only I'd known I could have asked you back at the shop, dear God, I have wasted so much time." He stood abruptly and paced the room.

"Hilda?" she said quietly. "Hilda Perry?"

Angus spun where he stood and stared at her.

"Oh Angus, Hilda is the friend I speak of. Hilda is the one they have called a bolter." June was starting to speak fast. "I went to see the matron at the hospital, and she told me that it was indeed Hilda that had been taken by Mr Drake, and that there was talk in the town that he would treat her mercilessly." June rushed over to Angus. "You must ride out there Angus, out to his settlement before he hurts her."

"Why would he want to hurt her?" Angus was starting to get heated.

"He took an unnatural liking to her on the ship. Nothing happened at the time, but having her to himself will be different. Ride out there now, hurry."

27

Angus rode behind Michael, appreciating his speed and direction. They rode the horses hard for a day and a half, stopping only to rest for the night. Michael told Angus stories of Captain Drake that made his blood boil, pushing him on faster.

When they finally made it to the Drake property they found it abandoned. The doors were open, and looters had been through. There were no animals left in the fields and the horse stalls were empty.

Angus stormed around the house looking for any sign that Hilda had been here, and found nothing. He went out to the barns and found a small room where prisoners had been chained to the walls, iron collars lay scattered on the floor and long tendrils of hair were caught in the rough timber walls. His mind went berserk, and a rage grew in himself that could not be contained. He ran out into the yard and came face to face with two soldiers, pistols drawn, standing in front of a genteel man.

"What is the meaning of this!" the genteel bellowed. He was stumpy and round with a long grey wig on his head. "Looters, shoot them!"

Angus held up his arms to try and calm the situation, when one of the soldiers recognised him.

"Hey, you are the bar tender from the Inn. What are you doing out here?"

Angus lowered his arms and started walking towards them, forcing them to back up and hold their pistols higher. "Wait, please wait. Let me speak."

He turned and showed them he was not carrying any weapons. "I came here looking for the woman you spoke of last night," he finally said.

"What! The bolter?" the soldier said and lowered his pistol. "What you want with her?" he asked.

"She was a friend of mine, back in England. When you spoke of who had charge of her, I got worried and came to see if she is all right." He looked around at the homestead then back to the genteel. "Is she all right?" he asked softly.

The genteel pushed past the soldiers and told them to lower their weapons. "My name is Sir Thomas Holdings," he extended his hand to Angus who introduced himself. "This property belonged to my daughter and her wretched husband, Captain Drake. I'm not sure what went on out here, my daughter won't speak of it. Drake is dead, and I cannot say I'm sorry about it. My daughter has gone back to England; I've come to organise the sale of the property."

"What of the convicts that worked here?" Angus did not care one bit for this man's woes.

"The ones still in service I have had released," he said pompously.

"Was there a blonde woman, tall with fair skin. Perhaps a little older?"

"Not when I came out here, I'm afraid." He pointed towards some trees up the back. "There are some graves up there I am told. Who is in them I do not know." Sir Thomas looked to the ground, slightly uncomfortable. "As I have said, Captain Drake was not a kind man."

Angus saw an elderly man walking up the driveway towards them and Sir Thomas turned to see where he was looking. "Ah, here he is. This is Mr Hardy; he used to be the groundsman. I have asked him to help me clean the place up for sale, in return for some household items." Sir Thomas turned and shook Mr Hardy's hand.

"Did you work here until the end?" Angus asked him.

He nodded and didn't speak but looked away from the glare in Angus's eyes.

"Did you see a blonde woman here? Is she still alive?"

The man nodded and pointed down the driveway, "She left with a small child." He pointed off into the forest. "They went north up the Cowering path."

"A small child?" Angus was mortified and wished he had the photo taken from Hilda's house. He described her in detail to Mr Hardy who nodded the entire time. Yes it was her, he said, and the child was not hers, just a broken kincher that had been left in the horse shed to die.

The soldiers were discussing going to look for Hilda as well, making Angus nervous. Would he kill them now to save Hilda. Yes he knew he would.

Angus looked to Sir Thomas "Sir, may I have your leave?"

"Yes, yes of course my good man. I hope you find her well." Sir Thomas turned to the soldiers and told them to leave the poor woman be, she had been through enough.

Michael was already standing behind Angus with the horse ready to go and they both mounted.

"She'll be looking for a doctor, Mr Drew," Mr Hardy said quietly before they left. "The child is near dead I am afraid." He looked to the ground after seeing the shocked look on Sir Thomas's face.

They cantered off down the driveway and came to a fork in the road "I know where the nearest doctor is Mr Drew, I will take you there." With that Michael pulled his horse to the left and dug his heels into its ribs making it race into the forest.

28

Angus and Michael rode hard through the forest until they came to the first river. They took a break to rest and water the horses, when Angus noticed some tracks in the river sand.

"There was a buggy and an old horse here," Angus pointed to the tracks.

"Old horse?" Michael questioned.

"The hoof print is heavy and shortly spaced, it was lame on one side." Angus followed the tracks deeper into the trees. "They camped here, she tied the reins to this tree, look." He was moving faster now, looking around the area. "There was another rider, here." He looked off towards the hills in the distance.

"That is the way to the doctors," Michael said and smiled. "Someone came to help them."

They both mounted their steeds and took off towards the mountain. It was a steep, rocky climb making them slow down, so they did not break the horses.

At the top of the mountain there was a flatter, grassed area with a hut off in the distance, smoke coming out of its chimney.

"It's the doctors house," Michael said jubilantly. And off they rode again.

Their approach must have been loud, for when they arrived at the hut a man in a suit was standing out the front with his rifle directed at them.

"Slowly now," he cautioned Angus as he dismounted.

"My name is Angus Drew, I am looking for the woman I love, Hilda Perry. Is she here with you?"

The doctor smiled and lowered his weapon. He stood to the side and opened the door further, allowing Hilda to walk out onto the steps. She took one look at Angus and burst into tears, running towards him. He lifted her off her feet into his embrace and held her tightly. Eventually, he put her down and cradled her head in his hands so he could get a good look at her. She was so thin and tired, and deep in her eyes he saw her horror and pain and he pulled her close again to his chest.

"I've come to take you home lass." He whispered.

Later that night they sat by the fire in the doctor's cosy hut. Hilda told Angus only the things she wanted him to hear, occasionally falling silent on the things she did not want to remember. Not yet. Angus let this moment go, he was not ready to hear it all, not yet.

"I've been working at an Inn run by your old friend June, now Mrs June Day," he eventually said, and she smiled with delight. "She said if I could find you she knew someone who could forge us enough documents to get you home." He was not sure if this was what she wanted. He prayed it was.

29

Hilda sat in front of the kitchen fire of June's Inn, the child on her lap sleeping, while she ran her fingers through her hair.

"She is lucky to not have any brain damage, Hilda, lucky that you turned up when you did. As awful as that may seem, you were her angel." June rose from her chair and moved to the cupboard to get them all another rum.

"I still can't believe Captain Drake is dead," June's husband sighed. "I did three voyages with the man, but he's done far worse than the two of you even know about."

"And by his own wife, no less," June added as she poured the drink into their mugs.

Angus could see Hilda was getting weary, and he stood and took the child off Hilda's lap and lay her by the hearth on the mattress June had made her. He pulled the warm rugs over her small form and looked up at Hilda. She had a sleepy maternal look in her eyes, staring down at the child, that made him want to take her home. "If you have a forger, June, why haven't you used him yourself," he turned and asked.

June looked at her husband and smiled. "I have a better life here than I ever had back in England." Her husband looked to the ground and blushed. "But you my friend," June addressed Hilda "Need to get back to England and get your revenge."

Hilda spoke for the first time, "I do not have the rage in me that I had at the start, June. The need for revenge is not as strong." Hilda ran her hand over her shaved head.

They all listened to her intently.

"I will not let it go, do not get me wrong. There must be retribution, and by God I will have it. I deserve it. But I just do not feel as angry." She took a sip of her rum and thought reflectively. "I feel sad for them. I know it sounds strange to hear, but what must exist inside of someone that they can be that selfish and destructive to rip apart a family? Not a happy person, not someone with any joy in their soul. It's not possible that people can hurt another so bad and then be happy."

"Aye," June said, "a deed so dastardly by two people could not bring joy to their home."

"But Missus," Mr Day added, "some peoples is just plain evil. I seen it in my soldiering days. They enjoy the nastiness they inflict on others."

"Yes," Hilda replied sadly, "I have seen plenty of that too. But surely when they lay their heads down to sleep, a darkness darker than the night must surely settle over their dreams."

"What will you do with them?" June whispered.

"I have thought of many things," Hilda smiled tiredly, "playful things that will satisfy my need for revenge without sending me back here for another seven years."

30

Hilda stood on the Portsmouth dock, hugging Eadlin until she declared she could not breathe. She stood back and wiped the tears from her eyes and remembered the wee child standing with her hand in hers staring up at them with fascination. Eadlin crouched down to the height of Rosie and adjusted her bonnet.

"Well, aren't you the prettiest little lady I have seen all day," she smiled at Rosie. "And what a lovely blue dress you have on. Where did you find such an outfit?"

"Aunty June took me into town and said I could pick any dress I wanted." She smiled up at Eadlin, deciding on the spot she was going to like this lady.

"Did you get the letters I sent from Rio?" Hilda asked intently.

"Yes mother, all six of them. It was quite the read." Eadlin laughed.

"I had a lot of time on my hands," Hilda smiled. "And have you managed to do most of what I asked?"

"Oh, mother, you are not a second off the boat and ready to reap your revenge. Tut-tut, I am but my mother's daughter," she laughed again, "of course I am ready."

Angus carried the cases over to Eadlin's carriage and secured them on the back, before turning and lifting Eadlin into an embrace.

"Thank you for bringing my mother home," Eadlin said.

"Yes well, now I just have to keep her alive for the next few days, then I think I have redeemed myself with your grandfathers' ghost." His laugh sounded as nervous as he felt. Hilda's next plan was probably going to be the death of him.

Eadlin handed her mother the valise with all her documents of identification. "I have found everything you need." She gave her mother one last embrace. "Take care mother, stay out of sight, word will travel fast that you are back in England if someone recognises you." Eadlin put her hand out for Rosie to take. "Shall we go for a ride, child, and you can see where I live. My housekeeper has prepared all sorts of delicious sweets for you; I think she plans to fatten you up." Rosie jumped in excitement and took Eadlin's hand to climb into the carriage. "Please take care, mother," Eadlin said over her shoulder one more time and smiled.

Angus hailed the next carriage, a sleek Landau model, fully enclosed for comfort in England's unpredictable weather.

"Where to Sir?" the coachman in the tall hat asked.

"Please take us to Lady Margaret Hashingham's in Knightsbridge, good man, and make haste." Angus settled Hilda in the carriage and put the throw over her legs. "Are you sure you don't want to give it a few days, get your strength back?" he asked her gently.

"There is no time, Angus. We cannot be seen by anyone, lest we lose the element of surprise." She put her hand on his leg and rested her head against his shoulder and fell straight to sleep.

Lady Margaret Hashingham, four-time widow and Knightsbridge's most influential gentlewoman, was renowned for her discreet problem-solving among the well to do. She was also a companion to Hilda's father for a short time after Hilda's mother had passed. Indeed, it was Lady Margaret who had loaned Mr Perry the downpayment for his Inn and given him a sly recipe for Laudanum Wine. Their gentle relationship had ended but they had remained friends till his passing. Lady Margaret was prudent in her speech and actions, especially to keep something confidential or to avoid embarrassment. Therefore, to Hilda it felt wise to seek her counsel on how to deal with her problems in a cautious yet satisfying manner.

The bouncing of the carriage on the city cobblestones woke Hilda from her rest. "Are we nearly there?" she asked sleepily and took a quick look out of the curtains. Rows and rows of beautiful white townhouses joined together, lined either side of the street, with columns and porticos out the front. Perfectly trimmed hedges and English roses demanded to be admired by the immaculately dressed ladies and gentlemen that walked by. So different from the world where Hilda had just come from, she thought to herself.

The carriage stopped, and Hilda's door was opened quickly by a doorman holding up a parasol. "My lady," he put a hand out to help Hilda down. "Lady Margaret is waiting in the library." He handed Angus the parasol to keep Hilda's face hidden and paid the coachman.

Inside the opulent foyer they were greeted by the maid and ushered upstairs to the library. Inside the fire was warm, and the décor was plush. Lady Margaret stayed in her seat; she did not feel the need to stand to greet people at her age but held out a hand for Hilda to take.

"My dear, dear Hilda!" she soothed. "What a terrible injustice you have been through, I just knew something was wrong, didn't I Bridgit?" She looked to her right at her maid, who was nodding supportively. She took Angus's hand next. "What a dear man you are, going to retrieve our Hilda, her father would have been most appreciative indeed. Sit, sit. Bridgit," she called to her maid. "Go get the good brandy dear, and we will see if we can get some colour back into Hilda's cheeks."

At exactly six-thirty on the dot dinner was served in the dining room. A delicate seafood bisque for starters, followed by Pheasant and artisanal English cheeses and for dessert some bread-and-butter pudding with aged rum. While Angus sat at the end of the meal sipping his vintage port and puffing on a cigar by the fire, Hilda was sure she was going to be sick after living on nothing but rations for a year.

They spoke of Hilda's father and the *special* wine he would make for Lady Margaret, and of her gratitude to Hilda and Angus for continuing the excellent work with much discretion. Hilda told her of her misfortune, and Lady Margaret sat in quiet, not interrupting even once.

"That is quite a story, my dear," Lady Margaret sighed, and held out her glass to Bridget for a refill. "I must say, I was surprised to receive the letter from your daughter and read it with great interest. The mere thought that the same could happen to myself, although everyone does know who I am so it most definitely would not, but the mere idea!" She put her hand on her chest for emphasis. "I knew straight away it was my civic duty to be of assistance. One does not get into the position that I am in society and fail to help the common people."

Hilda and Angus smiled to each other privately.

"You do us a great service," Hilda cooed, knowing full well Lady Margaret was bored as hell, and needed to get her teeth into something. Her father had disclosed some wily stories from her past; quite the artful conductor when one was in peril.

Lady Margaret finished her drink and stood with a groan that highlighted her years and called for Bridgit to assist her to bed.

She turned at the door and took one last look at Hilda. "We will discuss this further tomorrow my dear. Remember your journey, dear girl, and then you will remember why this must be done."

31

Moll Myrtle-Perry burst into the parlour with a recently delivered letter in her hand, waving it about and screeching for her housekeeper to attend her. She fussed about with her shopping, dropping it all over the floor, all the while yelling for William to come at once, making it near impossible for Mrs Booth to take Moll's coat and bonnet off.

"Oh, for pity's sake," she slapped the housekeepers' hands away, "useless old woman, just leave it, I will do it myself." She gave Mrs Booth a shove and proceeded to remove her own garments, still bellowing out for William, who was by now so over Moll's constant hysterics and drama, he rarely came to her call.

Strangely enough, life hadn't turned out as well as William had envisioned. Even though Moll had said she would be a better woman at taking care of him than Hilda, she had turned out to be far worse. Oh yes, the sex had been most accommodating and enjoyable at the beginning, but no sooner had they wed than the woman had changed altogether.

William felt deeply aggrieved for himself, and although he was now banned from going to the Men's Club by his new wife, he took respite there as often as he could knowing the women there understood his needs and sympathised with the neglect he endured. One shapely brunette had even suggested of late that perhaps he just needed a good woman that understood him better.

Moll stormed into the lounge and was furious to see William just sitting there reading his paper.

"William!" she yelled. "You insolent fool, I have been calling you!"

"Moll," he murmured, and slowly looked up at her with an innocent face, "I didn't hear you arrive. What exciting gossip do you have for me today?"

"Well, I never!" she stormed at him. "I do not gossip, William, I merely keep you updated on current affairs."

"Yes, quite." He raised his eyebrows and looked back to his paper.

Moll decided to carry on the argument later and walked over to the drinks table to pour herself a strong brandy. She waited several sips for William to ask her the news, but he never did, so she cleared her throat. "I have been invited to Lady Margaret Hashingham's for afternoon tea." She brushed at her skirts and smiled.

William looked up sharply with confusion. "Lady Hashingham's?" he questioned. "Why on Earth would you be invited to Lady Hashingham's?"

Moll was taken aback by his rudeness. "I will have you know, William, my place in society has elevated somewhat since I donated all Hilda's old stuffy furniture to the Ladies Auxiliary to raffle off, I should think news of my grand deed has made its way to Lady Hashingham." Moll sulked heavily into the settee and was annoyed to see William roll his eyes and go back to his paper. She thought to herself how he did that far too often these days. She looked across at him and admitted to herself that he wasn't really turning out as she had hoped at all. He had told her he was well off and influential, but the money from the sale of the Inn was already gone in necessary refurbishments of the house and her wardrobe. At least she had been clever enough to convince him into putting the titles of the estate in her name for safe keeping.

"My visit to Lady Hashingham's is this evening." She rose pompously and stared down at William, still reading his paper, and decided that perhaps she didn't really like him after all.

* * *

Lady Hashingham's carriage arrived promptly at three in the afternoon, and Moll was ecstatic to see the neighbours looking over their fences with curiosity. She slowly made her way from the front door to the carriage, much to the annoyance of the coachman, and waved to her neighbours in a queen-like gesture before alighting.

"Do go through the middle of town, sir, at a slow pace." Moll sat back in the plush chair and pushed the curtain right back to allow the full view of her presence.

The loyal coachman had been told by Lady Hashingham to do as the insipid woman requested on the journey home, and he would be rewarded for his patience with an extra bottle of rum. However, Moll's request to be driven slowly around the streets of Knightsbridge as well, had made their afternoon tea appointment unacceptably late, forcing Lady Hashingham to wait. And Lady Hashingham waited for no-one.

"Bridgit, please bring me a glass of my special wine, and be sure to hold me back when that ineffectual shrew arrives." Lady Margaret sighed and accepted the small crystal glass, making sure to just take a small sip. She needed her wits about her if she was to sit through this afternoon tea.

Lady Margaret sat upstairs and heard Moll arrive, in fact the whole house heard her arrive, and Lady Margaret rolled her eyes. Then there was the sound of the doorbell again, and as planned, Rupert Rumley had arrived. Rupert, Lady Margaret's nephew on her brother's side and right-hand man when it came to discreet meddling was always keen to be in on one of Lady Margaret's little schemes for the pure sport and enjoyment of it. Rupert Rumley was so rich he had nothing better to do. However, he was also put out at having to wait around the corner in his carriage for Moll's arrival and vowed to himself he would make her pay for such insolence.

As they were both escorted into the lounge, Lady Margaret could see instantly by the way Moll was blushing that her plan had begun. Rupert slid his way over to Lady Margaret, smooth and dashing and irresistible. He bent and kissed her hand, and they exchanged a sly wink. "By the heaven's, Lady Margaret, are you getting younger? You look ravishing."

"Oh, do stop, Rupert," she joked freely, "your smooth tongue doesn't work on me." She looked beyond Rupert to Moll and motioned for her to join them. They spoke for an hour of silly society things, making Rupert's life sound abundantly joy filled and carefree. Oh, the families they made up to make Rupert's lineage almost biblical, so much so that by the end of the tea, Moll was smitten.

She had mentioned along the way to Lady Margaret of her habituation for migraines, and did she have any suggestions? Of the whole exasperating experience of the afternoon tea, for Lady Margaret, this was the opening she had been waiting for.

"My dear, I have just the tonic." She turned and asked for Bridgit to get the bottle of Teasdale's Soothing Syrup and turned back to Moll with sympathy. "We women are under much duress in our day to day lives." She turned to her left and picked up a sheet of paper, handing it to Moll. "While Bridgit is gone, I would invite you to sign this," Lady Margaret tapped the piece of paper continuously with her pen to stop Moll questioning it. "It is a petition I am starting up for the women of society to be acknowledged for their endless work with the less fortunate. I've yet to give it a title" She handed Moll the pen and Rupert interjected.

"Such a worthy cause, Lady Margaret, I commend you," he preened. Moll looked at him and nodded, signing the paper immediately.

Lady Margaret snatched the signed paper off Moll while she was distracted by Rupert, and handed the sheet to Bridgit, then took the bottle of tonic off Brigit and held it out to Moll. She felt like she was selling a product as she held it. "All the women of high society are using this to soothe our nerves; I'm surprised you haven't heard of it?"

Moll turned the bottle over and read the back, "Laudanum, Indian Hemp, Morphine and Chloroform?" she looked up suddenly at Lady Margaret, who was annoyed the scamp could read.

"My dear, in such small amounts that even I myself have to take it several times a day, for it to even slightly calm my poor nerves." Lady Margaret pretended to be offended.

"Oh, of course, Lady Margaret. I wasn't suggesting anything of the sort. I will start taking it immediately, if you think it will help." Moll looked over at Rupert who was nodding in all seriousness.

"I think perhaps, being a much younger," Rupert winked at Moll, "and healthier woman, you may need to take a dash more for it to work. All the ladies in my family use it, bless their souls." He smiled his soft sexy eyes at Moll, and in that moment she would have drunk the whole bottle, had he asked her to.

"Can…can I see you again?" she stuttered, forgetting Lady Margaret was in the room.

"There would be nothing I would like more my dear." He looked to the ground as if aggrieved. "However, I cannot be seen with a married woman, my family simply would not allow it." Rupert took her hand, making her blush. "If only it were different." He stood abruptly and bowed to the women saying his goodbyes and swanned out the door.

32

Moll had been taking Lady Hashingham's tonic for nearly four weeks and was amazed at how it had relieved her migraines instantly but had noticed it gave her a slight dizzying effect after each dose. However, when she stopped taking it for even the first time, her migraines returned with a vengeance. She had become increasingly irritable with everyone around her, most of all William for his lack of sympathy and attendance and was prone to storming around the house and yelling expletives until someone located where she had left her bottle last. Eventually she found it easier to just keep it in her pocket, so it was available the moment she needed it.

She had thought she had overheard Mrs Booth say to the other staff that she wasn't taking enough, and this made her worry. She even wrote to Lady Hashingham for her advice, but hadn't heard back, so she demanded Mrs Booth go to the chemist to get several more bottles. She had decided perhaps she had heard wrong the dosage Lady Hashingham had suggested, and needed to increase how often she took it.

And then a letter had come for her one day from Rupert Rumley, asking after her and wishing to meet with her should she be able to steal herself away on the quiet. She kept the letter close to her and read it daily, until the day organised for the meeting.

They met in an out of the way Inn, and he spoke of his want to be with her over the flickering of the candlelight. He could see she had attempted to look desirable, but the black hollows and bags under her eyes made her look ghostly. She had gone to the ladies' room twice, and came back in a different temperament, but failed to curtail her rudeness to the bar staff. Her conversation was erratic at best, and she professed her love for him on several occasions, making him squirm slightly in his seat. They left the bar with a kiss and a promise to be together, if it were only possible.

Slowly, Moll became agitated and annoyed with how constantly tired she had become and demanded Mrs Booth send for the doctor. She didn't tell him about the tonic she was already taking, so he prescribed a mixture of mercury, iron and cocaine to counteract her fatigue, labelling her condition the "Drooping", and suggested she would be back on her feet in no time.

After two days, Moll's mind had become a bomb. She paced her bedroom in the middle of the night, chewing her nails till they bled. Back and forth she would pace in the dirty nightgown that Mrs Booth had tried to get her to take off so she could wash it, but it was her nightgown, not Mrs Booth's, and she would not let her steal her clothes. She had caught the cook, just a few moments ago, trying to steal food from the pantry, and she had hit her with a pan. This was her house, and she would not let them take it from her.

William made a snort from the bed, where he lay with a smug look on his face, and she turned on him and watched him. She had found the letters in his top drawer from the whore down at the Men's Club. How could he cheat on her, it was unthinkable. She went to the dresser and took a sip from both bottles, and bent over straight away, wincing from the stomach pain. Her body started to tremor, and a piercing pain shot through her lower abdomen. Then there was darkness.

She woke in the morning and found herself lying on the cold floor in an empty room. Her body stiff from the hard floor; her ear ached from being pressed to the slate. Still in her nightgown, damp with blood and sweat, she shivered and rose slowly. Her mind was spiralling, trying to recollect the night before, but nothing came to her. She looked to the bed for William, but he was gone, he must have stepped over her to leave the room. Her aching, cold feet padded through to her wardrobe, and she donned her gown, every movement causing ripples of pain through her body. She walked in a trance, hair askew, clothes hanging from her frame, half seeing, half blind down towards the staircase.

Halfway down the steps, Mrs Booth started to scream from the kitchen, where she'd just discovered the body, but Moll didn't stop. She walked into the dining room and went to the long mahogany display cabinet that lined one wall and opened the top drawer.

"What the blazes is going on here woman?" William rushed into the room behind her and started vehemently abusing her. What had happened to the cook, he demanded, and then on it went. The names he called her for letting herself go and not being there for him, how useless and unloving she was. On and on it went. Slowly she looked up and saw his reflection in the glass, all clean shaven and dressed to perfection. Where had he been this morning? Where was his care for her? She turned her attention to her own reflection and saw nothing but ruin. Slowly, she turned and raised the pistol that she had meant for herself and pointed it at William. His eyes grew large, and he raised his hands and started to back away.

"I don't want you anymore, William," she croaked and drew the trigger.

33

Hilda stood outside the room in the mental ward and watched Moll through the glass. She was bound in a white coat, its sleeves wound about her back, secured with belts. She sat in a corner rocking back and forth, occasionally looking up at Hilda and yelling something they could not hear through the glass.

"Seems her mind just snapped," murmured the doctor from next to Hilda, while he looked at Moll and shook his head. "Happens to a lot of women, you know. It's their weak temperance to life."

Hilda stiffened her shoulders, and Angus put his arm around her to keep her from reacting.

"What will become of her?" Hilda asked tersely.

"Here for the long stay, this one. Killed her husband and her cook. Right nut job. Can't send these ones to the colony, they're too unpredictable." He shrugged his shoulders, looked at Hilda's angry face confused, then just walked off.

"This wasn't meant to happen, not like this." Hilda eventually said to Angus.

"It was all going to plan until she called in the doctor." Angus sighed. "How were we to know she would take it so far?"

But Hilda knew, the thought had passed through her mind once upon a time.

Hilda stared at Moll for the last time, feeling no remorse or anger, even the pity was gone. Now she felt nothing at all. Time had patched her broken heart.

A wise woman once said, at a time of great pain, you must create a version of yourself that you need, to get through the war that you have been presented with. She will be strong and stubborn and resilient because she will need to fight the battle of survival. And eventually, this version of yourself will become someone you have to let go of as well. Because when mother time has released the pain and the weight that you have carried for too long, you must create a new version of yourself that does not live in the realm of fight and flight. You must let go of the strong version of yourself because she does not need to exist in this quiet place. The new version, the final version of you, must live in peace.

"Are you all right, Hilda?" Angus jolted Hilda out of her thought.

"Was any of this worth it? All the lies and misery and deceit." Hilda thought out loud.

"Yes," Angus said quietly "It has made you who you are today, right now. Free."

Hilda smiled and took Angus's hand in hers "Let's go start again, Angus. Let's go have another crack at making the finest fermentables this side of England."

Angus laughed at her impetuousness and shook his head. He put his arm about her shoulders and steered her away from the past.

THE END

Acknowledgments

Female Convicts Research Centre was a wealth of knowledge for me in my research. This is an amazing site run by volunteers to bring the stories forward for so many forgotten women.

> Australia Geographic.
> University of Tasmania
> Museum of History NSW
> National Library of Australia

I would like to thank my dear sister, Paula Van Bladel for her editing in what little time she had spare.

Jayden Morgan for putting up with my constant change of ideas on the cover.

And last but not least, Brendan Jackson for taking me to the pine plantations, where the air was clean and calming, and I could sit alone and listen as the trees whispered to me to carry on, no matter what.

Nieta Van Bladel is the author of the novels Hard Nor' West and Dead East and illustrator and author of several children's books including the Tilly and Dragadonna series. Born in Fremantle, Western Australia in the early seventies, Nieta spent much of her young life on the move with her mother and sister. After leaving home at the age of fifteen, Nieta set out to conquer the world. Her adult life was soon to mirror her childhood with her own two children. Raising them in towns from the far south of Western Australia to the Goldfields, before settling for eleven years in the Midwest town of Geraldton during the mining boom of the nineties. Uprooting again they moved straight through the centre of Australia to the East coast and back again several years later. This semi-nomadic life inspired Nieta to use the magnificent Australian landscape and open-road experiences to create memorable characters for her stories. Now a grandmother of two, Nieta is preparing for another lap around Australia as research for her next novel.

www.ingramcontent.com/pod-product-compliance
Lightning Source LLC
Chambersburg PA
CBHW030336010526
44119CB00047B/516